Hast Du Dich jemals gefragt, warum Hotelzimmer so selten die Orte sind, die man sich wünscht – an denen man gerne einschläft oder aufwacht? Kann es denn so schwer sein, ein Zimmer zu gestalten, in dem man wirklich gerne eine Nacht schlafen möchte?

Das für seine urbanen Interventionen bekannte Architektenkollektiv raumlaborberlin hat weltweit Architekturstudierende und Bastlergenies aufgerufen, das Hotelzimmer ihrer Träume für die Stadt Mannheim zu entwerfen. Eine international besetzte Jury renommierter Architekten und Künstler wählte aus den zahlreichen Einsendungen 22 Entwürfe aus, welche im Vorfeld des Festivals Theater der Welt in kleinen interdisziplinären Teams in einer öffentlichen Werkstatt vor dem Nationaltheater geplant, gebaut und anschließend an charakteristischen Orten, verteilt in ganz Mannheim, errichtet wurden.
Gebaut wurde mit wiederverwertbarem und gefundenem Material, nachhaltig und im offenen Austausch mit den Bürgerinnen und Bürgern. An den Grenzen von Architektur, Kunst, Design und sozialer Intervention entstand ein urbanes Laboratorium, das Fragen von kollektiver Umnutzung und Gestaltung der Stadt in eine gemeinsame Praxis umsetzt. Mannheimerinnen und Mannheimer sowie Gäste von außerhalb konnten während der gesamten Dauer des Festivals zu zweit oder allein in den temporären Installationen eine Nacht an einem besonderen Ort mit atemberaubender Aussicht verbringen und so einen neuen und fremden Blick auf die vertraute Stadt werfen.

Ferien in Mannheim!

Have you ever wondered why hotel rooms are rarely places you'd gladly fall asleep or wake up in? Is it so difficult to design a room where someone would enjoy spending a night?

raumlaborberlin, the architect collective famed for its urban interventions, has called upon architecture students and gifted DIY cracks worldwide to come up with the hotel room of their dreams in Mannheim. An international jury made up of renowned architects and artists has picked 22 winning designs. From mid-May on, the winners built each of their rooms at different locations in the city where they were open to guests over the period of the 17 days of the festival Theater der Welt. The central hub was Mannheim's Nationaltheater: from the open workshop located here, the construction teams spread out into the city.
Reusable or found material was used in the construction; sustainable and planned in an open exchange with Mannheim's residents. At the interface between architecture, art, design and social intervention, an urban laboratory was created where questions of converting collective space and urban design were implemented in collaborative practice. The residents of Mannheim and guests from abroad were invited to spend a night in the temporary installations alone or in pairs, in a special place with a breathtaking view, and see their familiar city from a new, unusual angle.

Holidays in Mannheim!

Whoofo

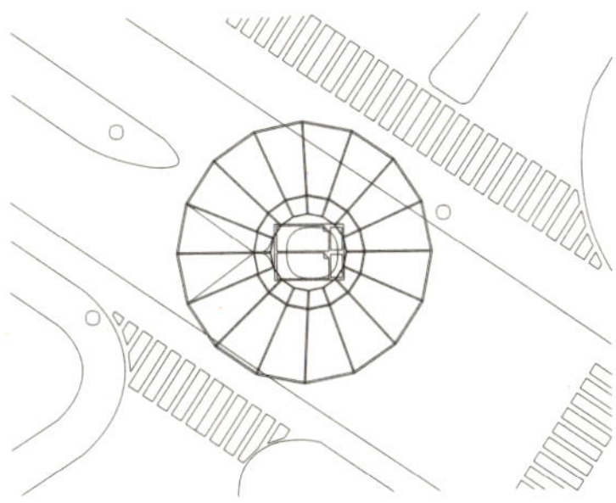

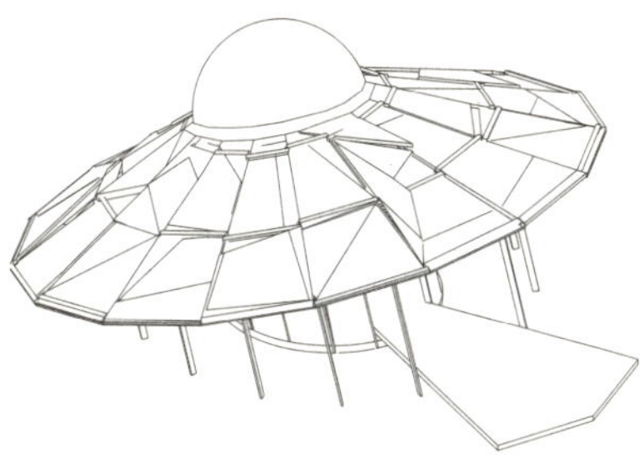

Team
Thomas Quack, Alain Yimbou, Benjamin Nast, Jan Bertil Meier, Aljosha Höhborn

From
Düsseldorf / Germany

Spot
Benjamin Franklin Village, Street Crossing

Materials
Roof laths, OSB, scrap metal, space suit

Specials
A view of the stars as you fall asleep. Special item: space suit (if you are picked up by extra-terrestrials).

01

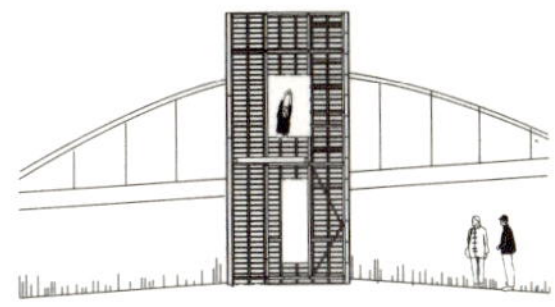

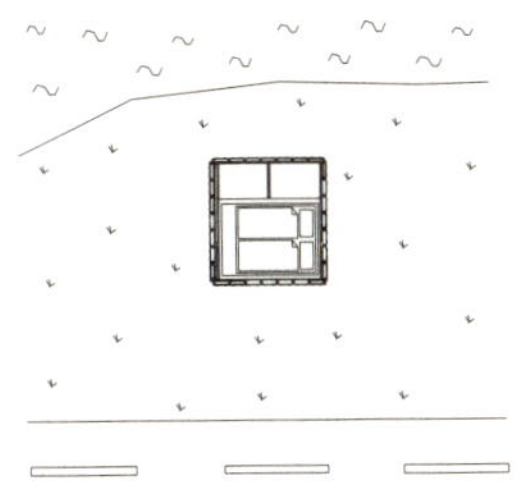

Living Room for the City

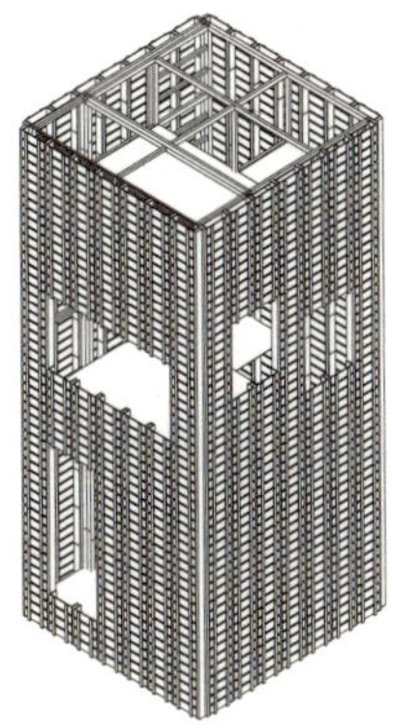

Team
Jennifer Gutteridge, Alex Butterworth, Katherine Nolan, Claudia Fragoso

From
Cambridge / UK

Spot
Neckarvorlandstraße / Verbindungskanal

Materials
Steel construction from stage set, wine crates

Specials
Constructed using a truck-mounted crane, anchors hammered in by the structural engineer himself

02

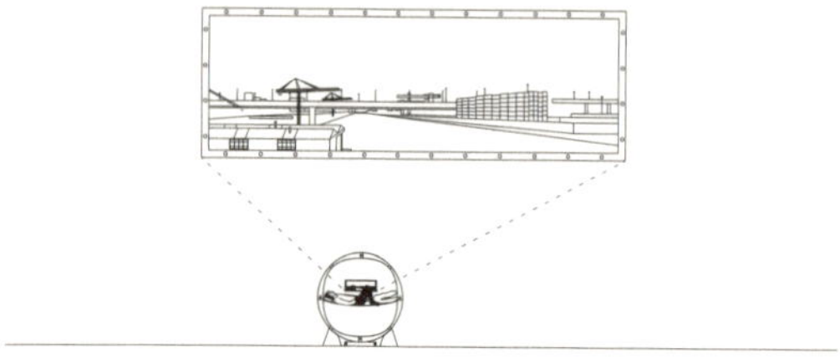

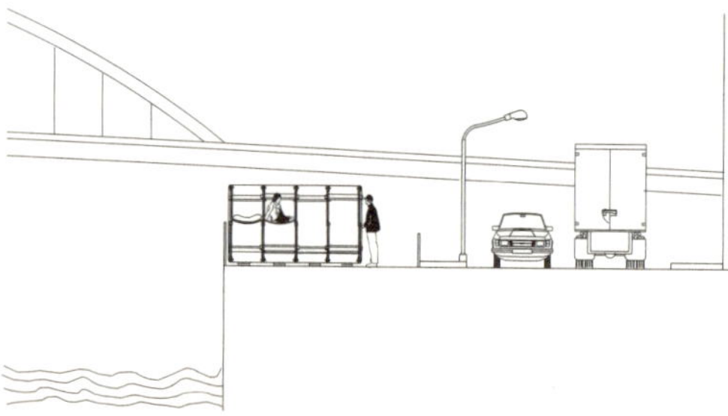

Tubheim

Team
Benoit Gavard, Pierre Yves Baron, Glenn Desury, Audrey Vongdara, Alexandre Andre

From
Normandie, Bretagne/France, Belgium

Spot
Regattastraße

Materials
Tarpaulin, linen, wooden stage boards

Specials
Winner of the online vote, construction solely using plug connectors, completely without screws.

03

For'rest

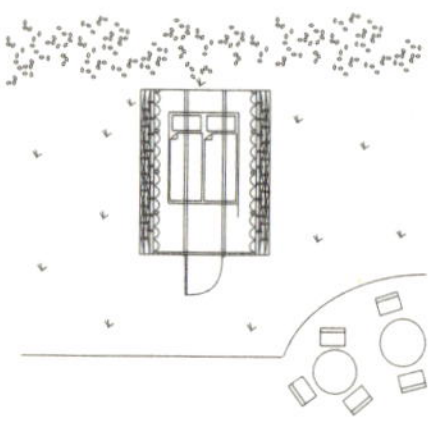

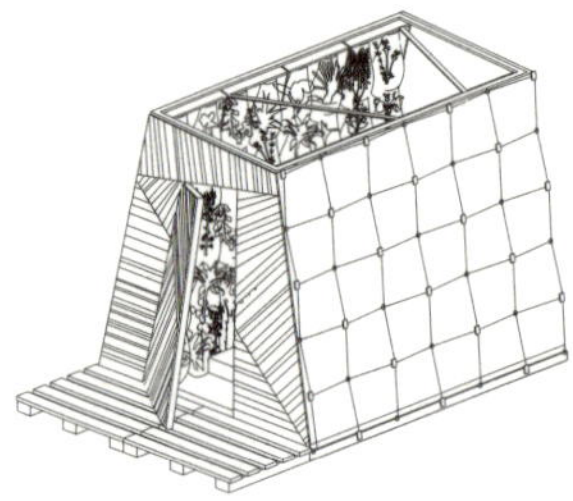

Team
Iga Kolozdiej, Anka Zawadzka, Jan Dowgiatto, Przemek Wos

From
Gedansk, Warszawa/Poland

Spot
Rosengartenpark; backyard of Dorint Hotel

Materials
Wooden posts, jute, potato sacks, plants from the Benjamin Franklin Village

Specials
Hybrid of a hotel room and garden, room service and wellness area.

04

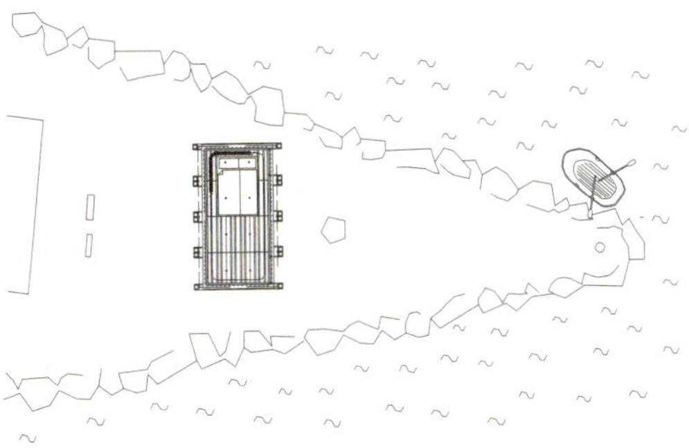

The Hedonist

Team
Nuno Pimenta and Frederico Martins with Miguel C. Tavares, Ricardo Leal and Rui Manuel Vieira

From
Porto / Portugal

Spot
Neckarspitze

Materials
Pallets, stay braces, corrugated PVC panels

Specials
The furthest view, the most transparency.

05

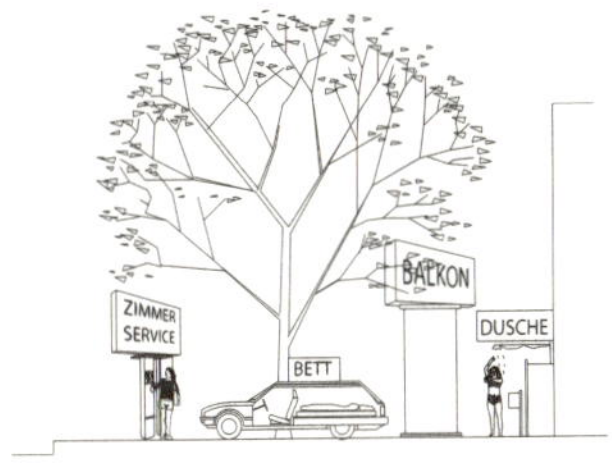

Hotel Carl

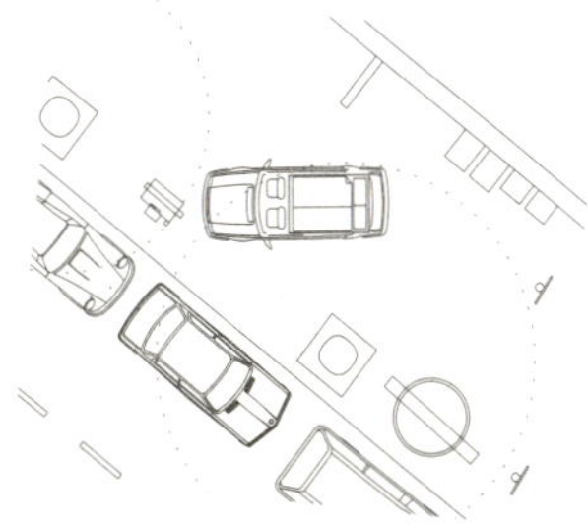

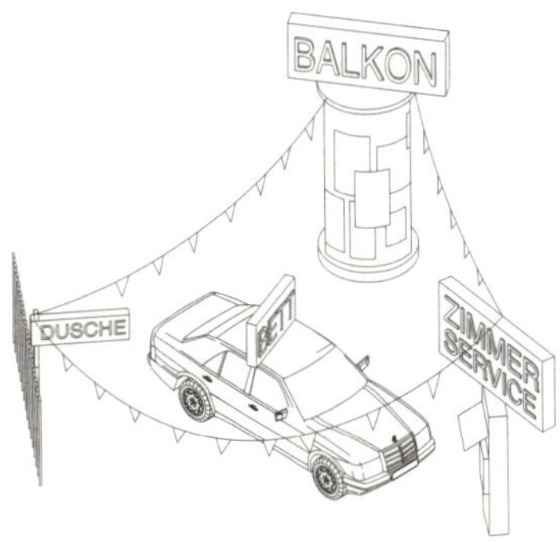

Team
Derk Thijs, Vanessa Gutberlet, Vera Egli, Marc Warrington, Fjolla Rizvanolli, Luana Paladino

From
Zurich / Switzerland

Spot
Otto-Beck-Straße / Seckenheimer Straße

Materials
Car, black and white plastic film, pieces of material

Specials
Conversion of city amenities into a hotel room.

06

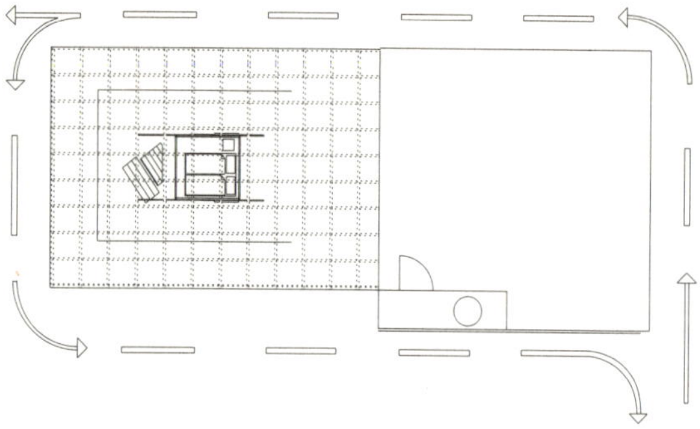

Fast Sleep Restaurant

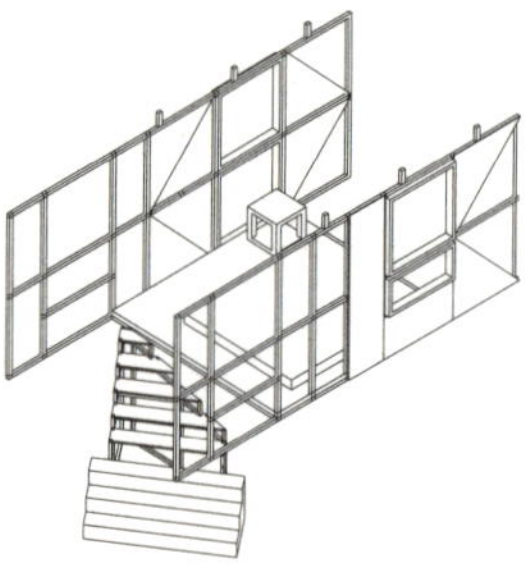

Team
YA+K; Yassine Elkherfih, Anouk Goelo, Pascal Osten, Alexis Gouin, Eric Peixe, Mascha, Timothe

From
Paris / France

Spot
Benjamin Franklin Village; abandoned Burger King

Materials
Left overs from old set designs from the opera, elements from unused playgrounds of the deserted and closed Benjamin Franklin Village, used Burger King restaurants

Specials
High spine-chilling potential (but elegant at the same time).

07

Monumotel

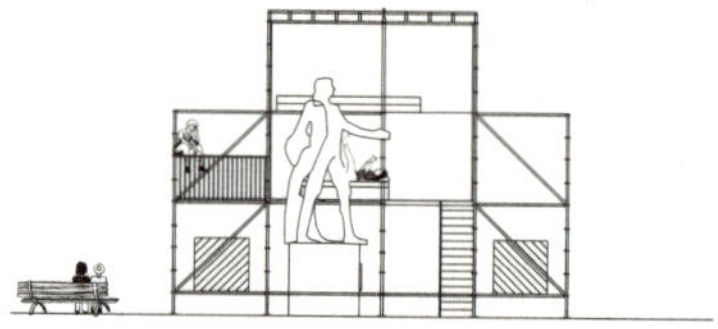

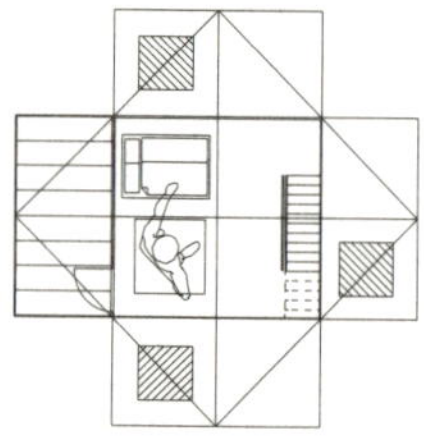

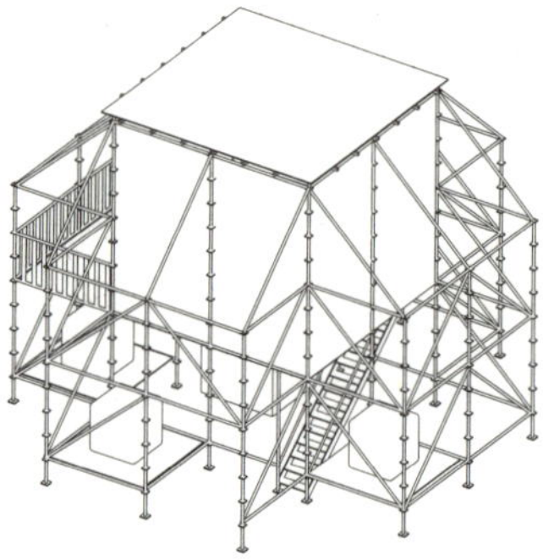

Team
Daniel Segerberg, Verena Resch, Georg Schwarz, David Edward Allen, Munan Ovrelid, Max Frey

From
Berlin (ehem.Trondheim, Wien, Graz, Suffolk etc.) / Germany

Spot
Schillerplatz; Schillerstatue

Materials
Schiller, scaffolding, mesh banner of the NTM programme

Specials
The hotel room with the most valuable interior.

08

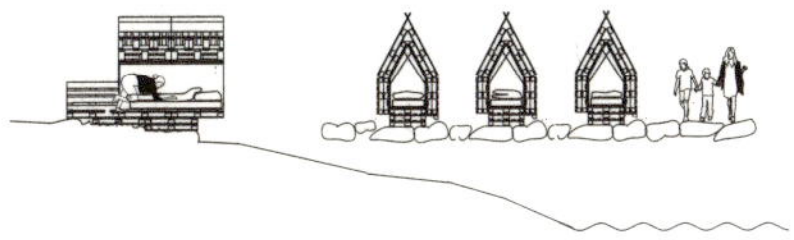

Collini Bay Resort

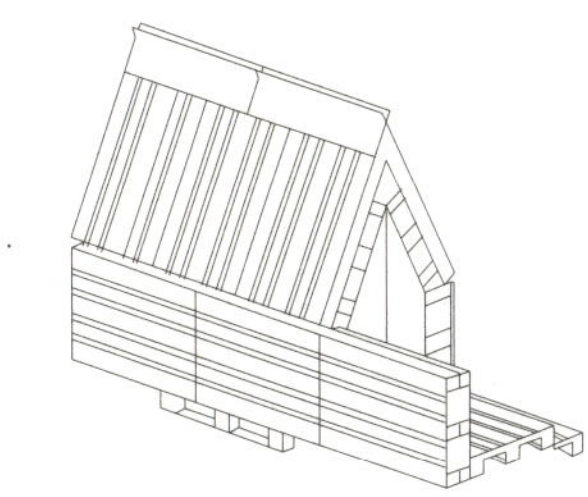

Team

Yalla Yalla! Robin Lang, Wulf Kramer, Timo Amann

From

Mannheim / Germany

Spot

Neckarpromenade

Materials

Pallets, yellow paint

Specials

The largest sleeping capacity: 3 rooms so 3 beds; the only local team, and the best party location.

09

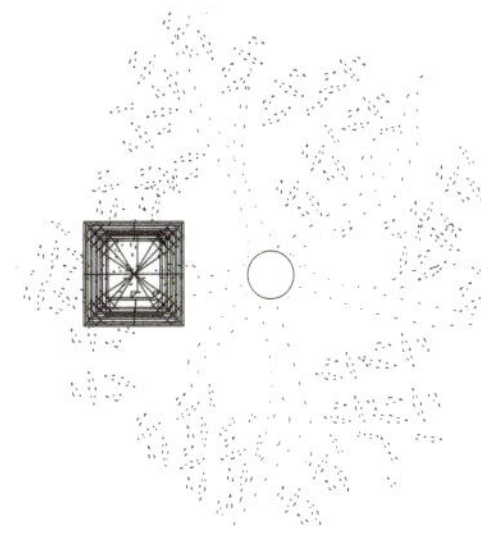

Zum Goldenen Flaschenzug

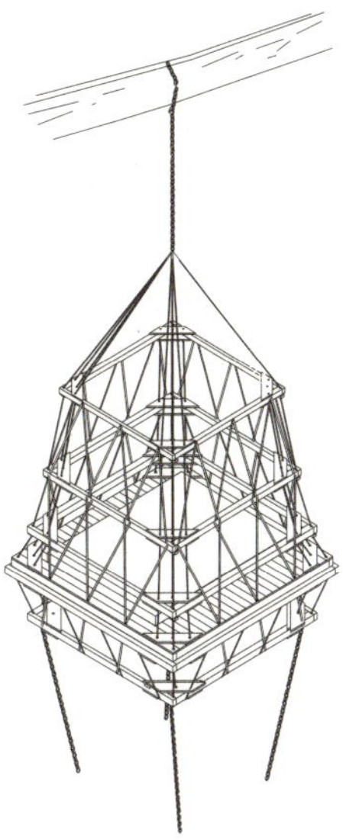

Team

Clemens Bauder, Felix Ganzer, Maximilian Ganzer

From

Linz / Austria

Spot

Luisenpark; Klangoase

Materials

Wooden posts, chain hoist, climbing rope, bicycle inner tubes

Specials

Hanging construction with wild parrots for pets.

10

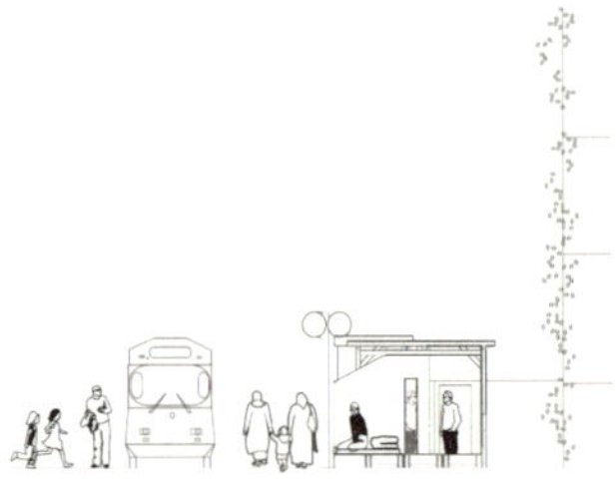

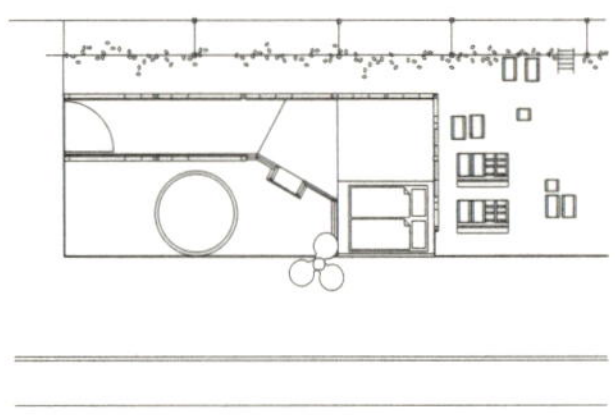

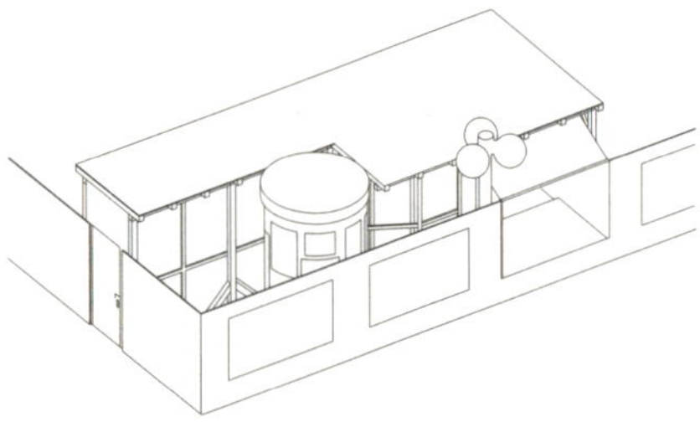

StattTheater

Team
Fabian Wolf, Luisa Rubisch, May Kukula, Tal Engel, Marius Schilling, Anna Derricks

From
Berlin / Germany

Spot
Planken; Engelhorn

Materials
Molton frame from NTM, blockboard panels, reflective foil

Specials
Hiding place behind a mirror in a construction fence – almost a magic trick.

11

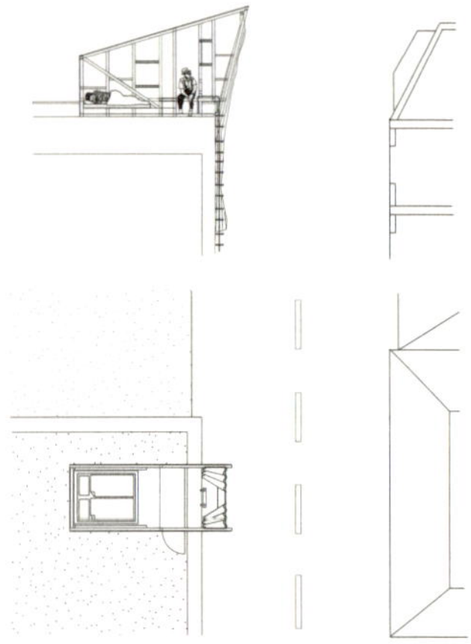

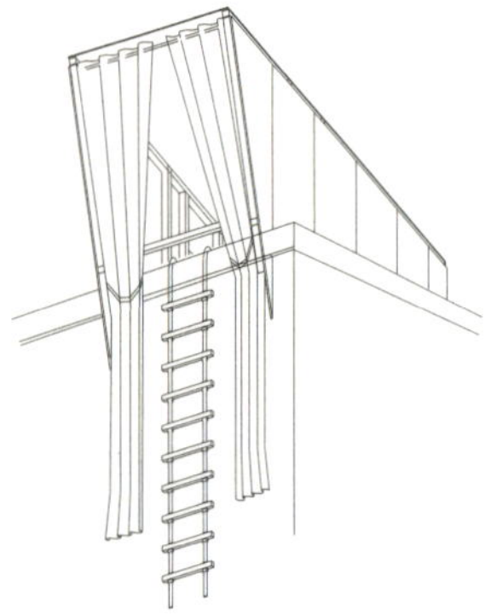

Stadtloge

Team
Kollektiv Kopfgemacht; Stephanie Nick, Franka Ismer, Johannes Dieckmann, Alexander Radomski, Daniel Gronau, Sebastian Witzke

From
Potsdam / Germany

Spot
Mozartstraße; Werkhausdach NTM

Materials
Disused set design material, opera foil, rope ladder

Specials
Use of the theatre technicians' pergola and barbecue areas, extremely dramatic drop height.

12

Schlafdom

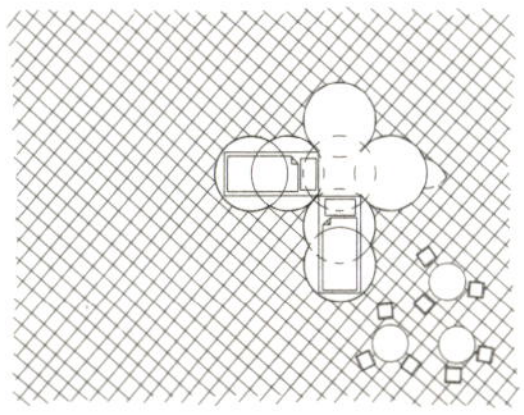

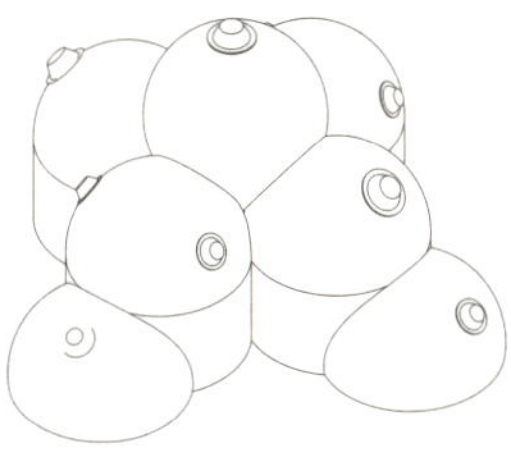

Team
Kollektiv Transtruktura; Wiebke Lemme, Nataliya Sukhova, Viktor Hoffmann, Andreas Heim, Vivian Schröder

From
Berlin / Germany

Spot
Marktplatz

Materials
Glass recycling containers, golden foil

Specials
Could be mass produced immediately (the material is available).

13

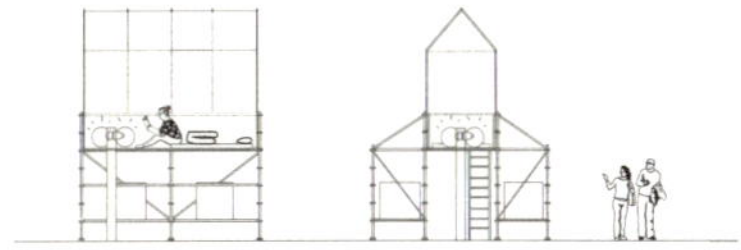

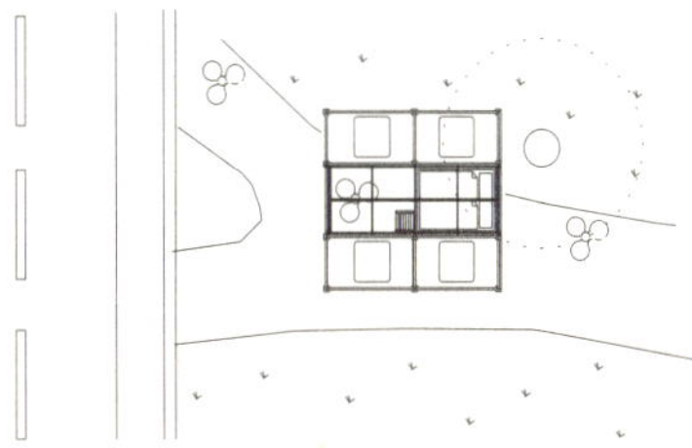

3-Lichter-Hotel

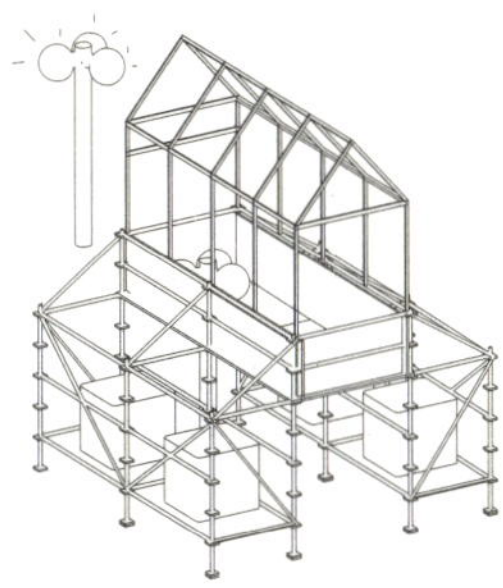

Team
des singes en hiver; Nathalie Fournier, Cecile Roturier, Pablo Ruamps, Simon Durand, Benjamin le Roux, Mathieu Le Roux

From
Paris / France

Spot
Neckarpromenade; Laterne

Materials
Streetlamps, scaffolding, wooden posts and planks, corrugated PVC panels

Specials
Nightlight included (slightly outsized light switch).

14

Prinz Käse

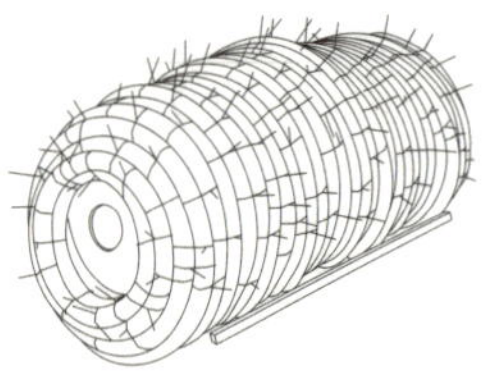

Team
Morgenwirdsbesser; Kristina Szeifert, Gizzem Cinar

From
Karlsruhe, Berlin / Germany

Spot
G7 Innenhof

Materials
Drainpipe, wooden posts millions of crable strips

Specials
Capsule hotel room with Japanese dimensions (very cosy).

15

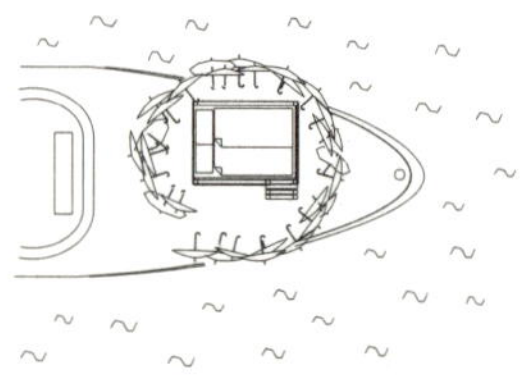

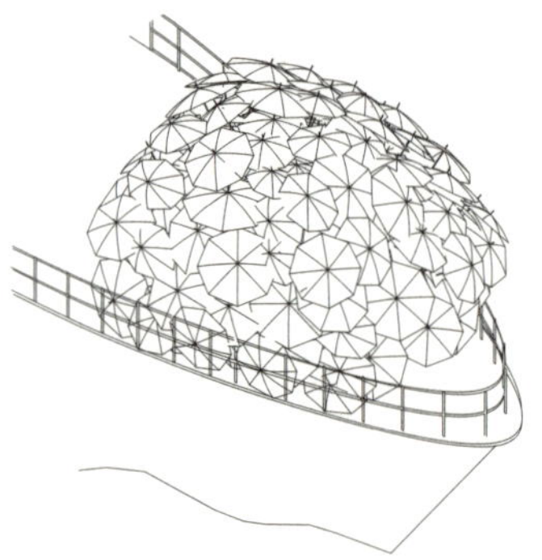

Under my umbrella

Team
Janine Ganserich, Heinrich Altenmüller, Mathias Komessker, Jan Grüneberg, Alex Terres, Arni Tolnai

From
Aachen / Germany

Spot
Museumsschiff

Materials
Umbrellas, wooden posts

Specials
The most intimate contact to Mannheim locals (every umbrella was from a different shop), minibar.

16

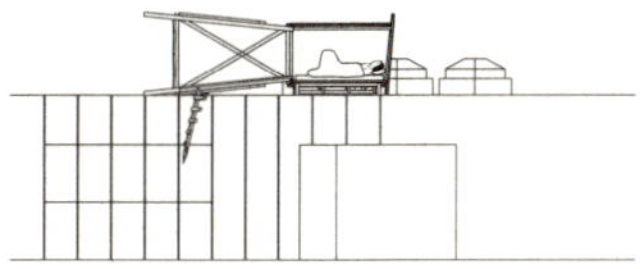

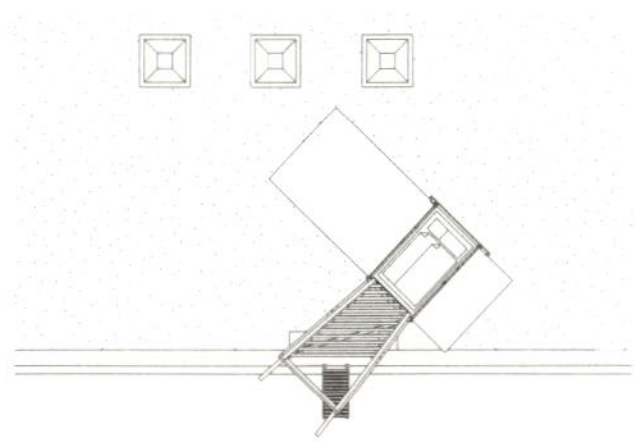

Mama Peter Löres

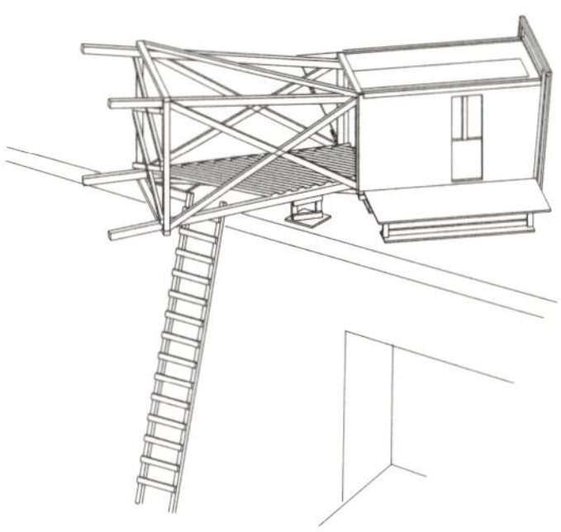

Team
Marian Korenika, Nele Faust, Victoria Philip, Carlo Siegfried, Alexandra Besta, Alper Kazokoglu

From
Karlsruhe / Germany

Spot
Augustaanlage; Dach des Kunstvereins

Materials
Raised hide

Specials
Hotel room used the material of the groups 2013 art campaign at the Mannheim Museum of Modern Art.

17

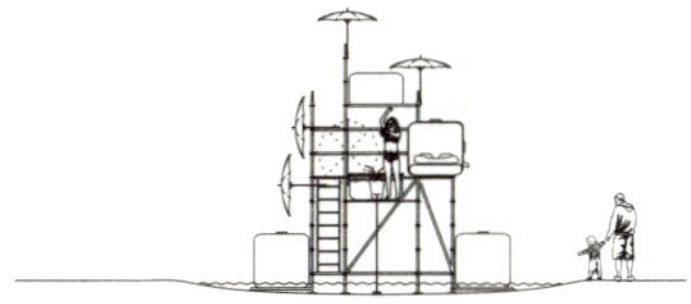

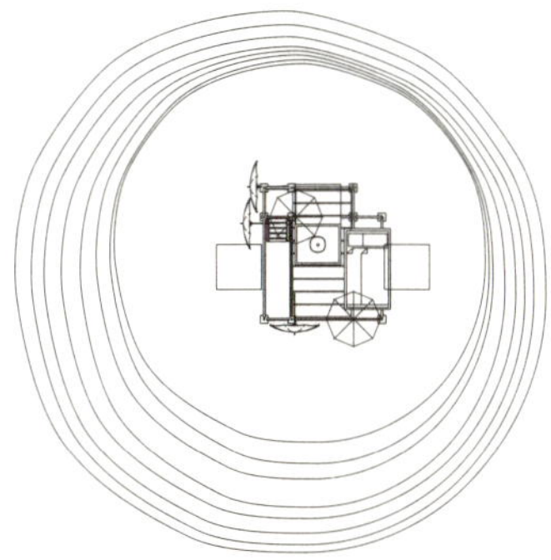

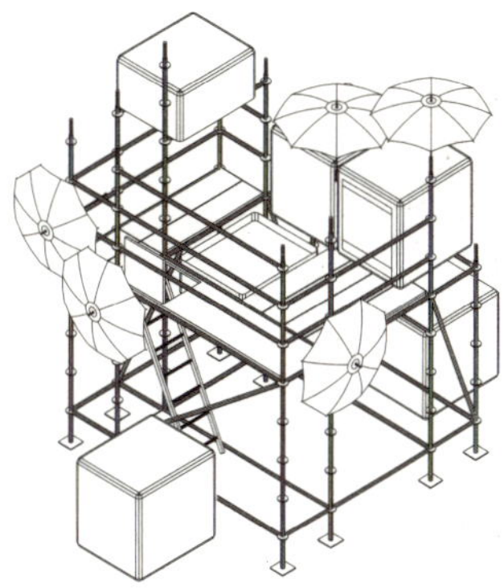

Fairy Tank

Team
Pierre Yves Guérin, Rozenn Balay, François Vaugoyeau

From
France

Spot
Herzogenriedpark; Springbrunnen

Materials
Scaffold, water tanks

Specials
A fountain as an alarm clock (from 8 o'clock) and an entire park as a private terrace (until 8 o'clock).

18

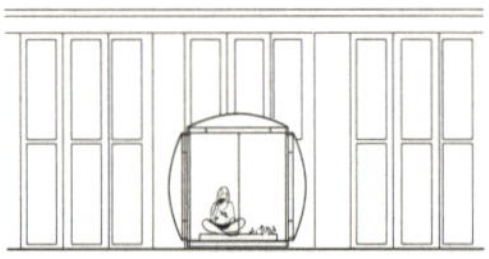

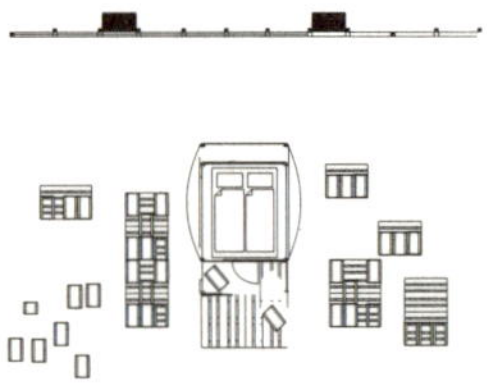

11-Uhr-Nachts

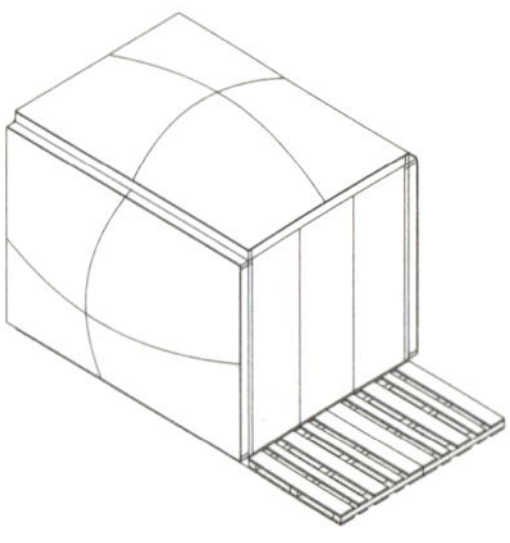

Team
Adriano Hellbusch, Jan Wind, Daniel Vedder

From
Berlin / Germany

Spot
Gottlieb-Daimler-Straße; Großmarkthalle

Materials
3 skylights, wooden posts and planks

Specials
Minimalist materials used to great effect after the largest initial difficulties.

19

RE:RE:AW

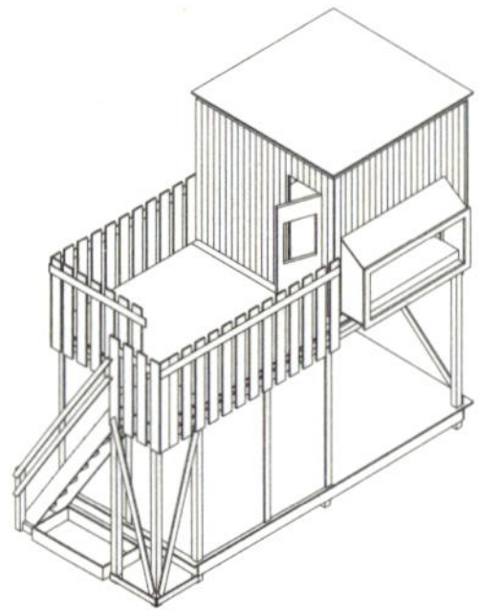

Team
Adrian Pöllinger, Jonathan Banz mit Jugenkulturzentrum FORUM, Mannheim

From
Zurich / Switzerland

Spot
Turley Barracks

Materials
2 saunas, concrete foundation, wooden posts and planks

Specials
With the collaboration of Mannheim teenagers, a hotel room was built that could be put to further use straight away.

20

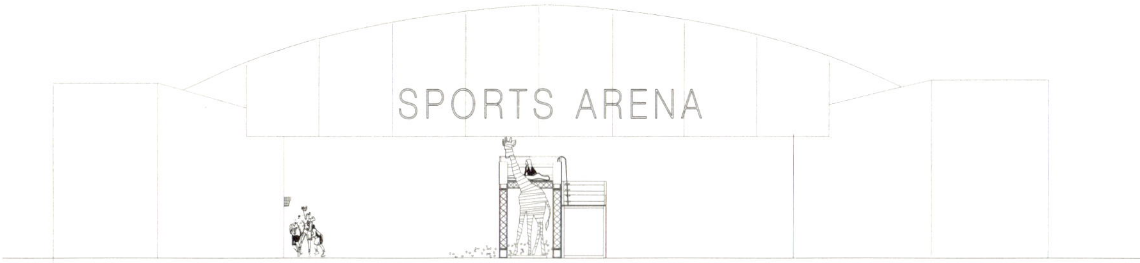

Feuer und Flamme

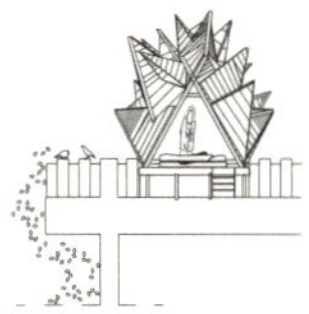

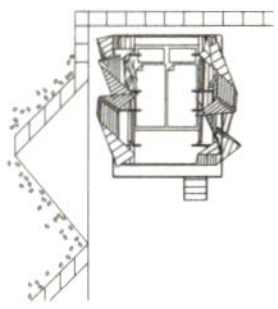

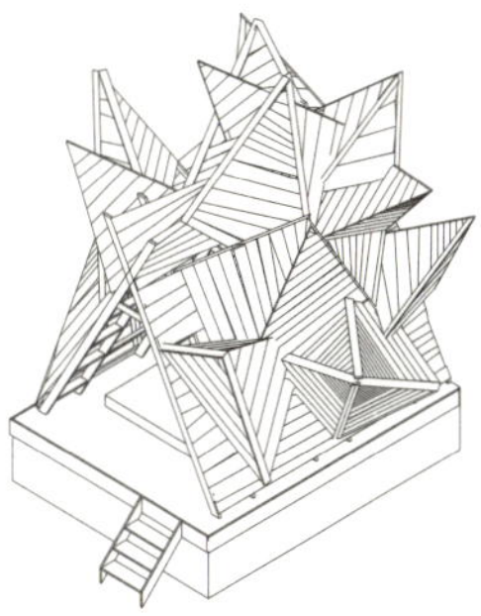

Team
Jacob Frisch, Maria Hofmann, Katharina Haeffner, Lukas Meier, Carolin Reinhardt, Christine Siebert

From
Schneeberg, Thüringen / Germany

Spot
Parkhaus N2

Materials
Wooden posts, stage podium, fire brigade hoses

Specials
Hotel room as a landmark visible from far and wide, with planned re-recycling of the material.

21

Sportsarena

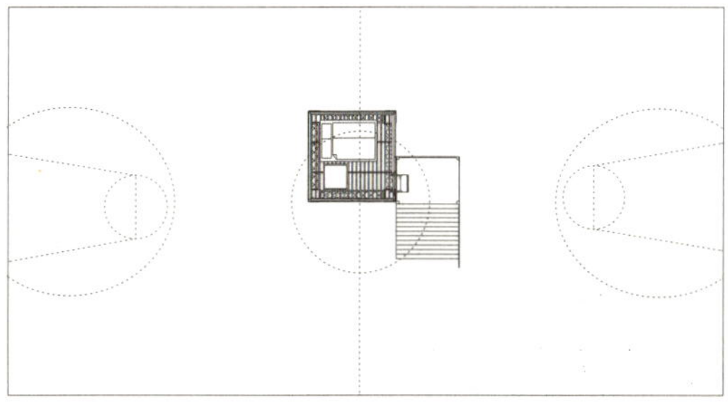

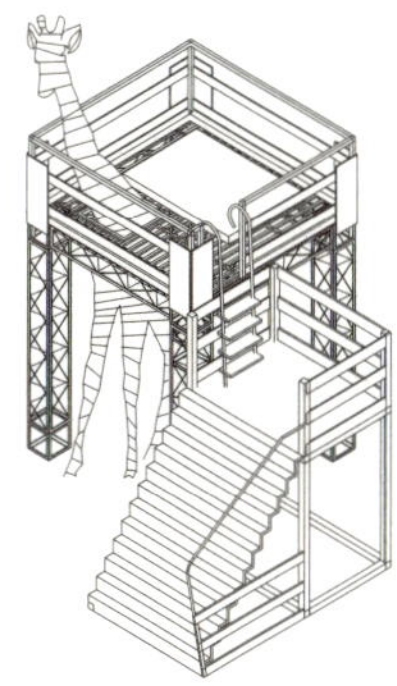

Team
YA+K; Yassine Elkherfih, Anouk Goelo, Pascal Osten, Alexis Gouin, Eric Peixe, Mascha Fehse, Timothé Osten

From
Paris / France

Spot
BFV Sportsarena

Materials
Squared timber tower, giraffe

Specials
The largest hotel room, and only room with electricity and floodlight.

22

MAIN-MOBILIA

Oh nein, jetzt zieht er seine Knarre...

Benjamin Foerster-Baldenius
raumlaborberlin,
Künstlerische Projektleitung
HOTEL shabbyshabby

Ich mag Mannheim, weil es so unberechenbar ist. Seit ich in der Stadt arbeite, passieren mir Dinge, die mir sonst nirgendwo passieren. Man denkt ja, Mannheim sei so eine spröde, provinzielle Schönheit, eine noch recht funktionierende, westdeutsche Industriearbeiterstadt – und das ist auch richtig. Hier gab es – wie in vielen Städten – ein paar gesellschaftlich-kulturelle Größen, die man mühsam zur urbanen Marke entwickelt: Friedrich Schiller war mal da, nun gibt es am Nationaltheater die Schillertage. Xavier Naidoo ist hier aufgewachsen, nun gibt es die kleine – aber einzige – deutsche Pop Akademie. Carl Benz hat hier das Auto erfunden und hat bis heute Arbeitsplätze hinterlassen. Und SAP wurde hier in der Region gegründet und hat es von hier aus zum größten Softwareunternehmen Europas geschafft. Nun hat einer der Gründer für 50 Mio. Euro eine neue Kunsthalle spendiert. Aber all das will nicht so richtig reichen, um Mannheim zum Favoriten auf den Titel der Europäischen Kulturhauptstadt zu katapultieren. Dabei müsste man nur genau hinsehen, und würde viel mehr entdecken, denn Mannheim ist die Stadt der kleinen kuriosen Wunder:
Wir sind in der Stadt, in der ein amerikanischer GI mit einem Panzer vor Liebeskummer Amok gefahren ist, um am Ende samt Panzer von der Kurpfalzbrücke in den Neckar zu stürzen. Hier bastelte Prof. Mo Edoga Jahrzehnte hinter dem Kunstverein in seiner Himmelskugel aus Treibholz herum und hielt jedem vorbeigehenden Interessierten einen Vortrag über zeitgenössische Kunst (nun ist er gerade gestorben). Als ich das erste mal Mannheimer Boden betrat und mich gerade über die Adresse wunderte, die ich nun aufsuchen sollte (alles was da stand war E7), wurde ich fast von einer Hundertschaft Harley-Rockern überrollt, ich vergaß darauf mein Frühstück bei der Bäckerei Grimminger zu bezahlen (Cappucino + Croissant + Brötchen + Butter + Käse + Marmelade + Saft = 3,95 €!) und verlief mich dann in den Quadraten. Im Jungbusch-Viertel traf ich mich endlich mit zwei Freunden, da kam ein Typ mit Schlangenlederschuhen des Weges, der mit seinem Tabletcomputer am Ohr telefonierte. Sobald er uns sah, zuckte er zusammen und brüllte in sein iPad „Ey! Du glaubst es nicht! Ich steh vor der Inkarnation von Starsky und Hutch, ja, die aus der Fernsehserie! Aber wer ist der dritte Typ? Oh nein, jetzt zieht er seine Knarre…" Ich gab ihm meine Kamera, damit er ein Foto von uns vor einem Italo Café macht und er zückte seine Visitenkarte, auf der stand „the most hated photographer of the world". Als ich nachts zu meinem Hotel in E7 schlenderte, hielt mich eine Gruppe junger Leute auf, die sich einen Sperrmüllhaufen zum Freiluft-Wohnzimmer drapiert hatten und alle Passanten zum Getränk einluden. Ich blieb ein paar Stunden dort und ging weiter meinen Sozialstudien nach. Am nächsten Morgen, ich war noch nicht ganz wach, erinnerte mich die Bäckersfrau freundlich an meine offene Rechnung. Zugegebenermaßen gibt es überall Freaks und spezielle Charaktere, aber selten ist

mir eine Stadt wie Mannheim begegnet, in der die Stilblüten so dicht neben der Straße wachsen.

Mannheim ist eine Stadt, der eine große Transformation bevorsteht. Während überall auf der Welt die Hafengebiete zu neuen Stadtentwicklungsflächen werden, weil Gütertransport heute andere Bedingungen braucht als vor 100 Jahren, ist hier noch der größte Binnenhafen Europas aktiv. Während in vielen europäischen Städten der Einzelhandel in der Innenstadt bankrott geht, weil Waren nicht mehr durch Schaufensterauslagen vermarktet werden, hat Mannheims Einkaufsstraße den größten Umsatz Deutschlands. Die großen öffentlichen Bauten wurden um die 1970er Jahre herum gebaut und werden gerade alle gleichzeitig baufällig. Allen voran das in den 1950er Jahren gebaute Nationaltheater. Der Beton ist porös, die Technik veraltet, die Kapazität zu groß. Das technische Rathaus ist so marode, dass es abgerissen werden muss, die Multihalle ist schon seit fünf Jahren geschlossen und die Kunsthalle wurde gerade abgerissen. Ganz zu schweigen vom Zustand der Rheinbrücken, aber die hat ja Ludwigshafen bezahlt. Und die Liste geht noch weiter: Nach dem Abzug der amerikanischen Truppen stehen zehn Kasernen mit insgesamt 526 Hektar Land und schätzungsweise 500 Gebäuden leer und suchen nach neuen Ideen. Für diese Aufgabe hat die Stadt eine eigene Behörde erfunden, die Kulturelle Stadtentwicklung heißt und einen Prozess moderiert, der sich bemüht, die Stadt in ein neues Zeitalter zu manövrieren. Und schließlich der öffentliche Raum: Mannheim ist nach dem 2. Weltkrieg als Autostadt entwickelt worden. Breite Straßen, riesige Brücken, dunkle Unterführungen und aufwändige Parkleitsysteme dominieren die urbanen Freiräume. Radfahren in Mannheim ist kein Vergnügen. Die fortschrittlichen Städte in Europa reduzieren sukzessive ihre Parkplätze, führen Fahrradstraßen ein und verbessern den öffentlichen Nahverkehr. Was soll Mannheim mit all diesen Flächen anfangen, wenn es bald keine Autos mehr gibt? Früher hat man geschliffene Festungsanlagen einfach zu Parks umgestaltet, aber Grünanlagen gibt es hier ja schon viele. Mannheim steht eine sehr bewegte Zukunft bevor.

Und genau hier setzt HOTEL shabbyshabby an. Das Projekt ist nämlich eine als Theaterfestivalprogramm getarnte Stadtentwicklungsrevolution in homöopathischen Dosen. Kleine Hüttchen die – wie Nadeln an der richtigen Stelle aufgestellt – eine neue Welt eröffnen. Nicht nur ein anderer Blick aus der Hütte auf die schöne Stadt, mit dem man das, was schon immer da war, neu sieht, sondern der Blick durch das Schlüsselloch auf eine andere Zukunft. Eine Stadt, die vielleicht morgen ganz anders funktioniert; in der der öffentliche Raum nicht die Fläche zum Durchqueren von einem Ort zum anderen ist, sondern ein Ort, in dem Stadt entsteht und verhandelt wird. Wir wollen die kleinen Shabbys als Prototypen sehen für Räume, in denen die MannheimerInnen ihren Spleens freien Lauf lassen können, und zwar so, dass es alle mitbekommen und anderen den Mut geben, nachzuziehen und so die Stadt zu einer echten Metropole und Modellstadt der Alltagskultur zu machen.

Wir kommen wieder!

Oh no! he's pulling out his gun...

Benjamin Foerster-Baldenius
raumlaborberlin
Artistic Project Manager
HOTEL shabbyshabby

I like Mannheim because it's so unpredictable. Ever since I've worked there, things have happened that have never happened to me anywhere else. People think Mannheim is an austere, provincial beauty, a well-functioning, West German industrial town – and there's some truth in that. Here, like in many cities, hard work has gone into making a few big names on the socio-cultural scene into urban brands: Friedrich Schiller came here, so there's a Schiller Festival at Mannheim's Nationaltheater. Xavier Naidoo grew up here, so there's a small, but unique, German pop academy. Carl Benz invented the car here, and his legacy of employment has survived to this day. And SAP was founded in this region, succeeding as one of the biggest European software companies. The founder recently donated 50 million euros towards a new art gallery. But all this is not really enough to catapult Mannheim to the top of the European Capital of Culture list. However, when we look a bit closer, we discover so much more – because Mannheim is a city of small, strange miracles.

This is the place where a lovesick American GI ran amok in a tank, which ended with him plummeting from the Kurpfalz Bridge into the Neckar, tank and all. This is where Prof Mo Edoga tinkered around for decades in his Himmelskugel behind the Academy of Arts, holding lectures on contemporary art to any interested passers-by. (He has recently died). When I set foot on Mannheim's soil for the first time, scratching my head at the address I'd been told to find (the only thing on the paper was 'E7'), I was almost run over by a hundred-strong group of Harley rockers, making me forget to pay for my breakfast in the Grimminger bakery (cappuccino + croissant + bread roll + butter + cheese + jam + juice = 3.95€!), before getting lost in Mannheim's grids. In the Jungbusch Quarter, I'd finally caught up with two of my friends when a guy wearing snakeskin shoes came down the road, making a phone call with a tablet stuck to his ear. As soon as he saw us, he gave a start and yelled into his iPad, "Hey! You won't believe this! I'm standing in front of the reincarnation of Starsky and Hutch, yeah, from the TV series! But who's the third guy? Oh no, he's pulling out his gun…" I gave him my camera to take a photo of us in front of an Italian café, after which he whipped out his business card that read: "the most hated photographer in the world." When I was strolling back to my hotel in E7 at night, I was stopped by a group of young people who had turned a pile of old furniture into an open-air living room, and were inviting every passer-by to a drink. I stayed there for a few hours, continuing my social studies. The next morning, before I'd fully woken up, the bakery owner politely reminded me about my unpaid bill. True, there are unusual characters and freaks everywhere, but I've seldom experienced a place like Mannheim where the oddballs grow on trees.

Mannheim is a city about to undergo a major transformation. While in the rest of the world, ports are being redeveloped into new urban spaces because the transportation of goods has different requirements from 100 years ago, here one of the biggest inland ports in Europe is still in business. While in many other European cities, retail businesses in the city centre face bankruptcy because goods are no longer marketed in shop windows, Mannheim's high street still makes the highest turnover in Germany. Large public buildings were erected in and around the 1970s, all of which are now rundown, above all the Nationaltheater, which was built in the 1950s. The concrete is leaky, the technology outdated, the capacity too big. The Technisches Rathaus is so ramshackle that it has to be demolished, the Multihalle has been shut for five years, and the Kunsthalle has just been bulldozed. Not to mention the state of the Rheinbrücken, but Ludwigshafen picked up the tab for that. And the list goes on: after the American troops moved out, ten disused barracks sit stranded on a total of 526 hectares of land, and an estimated 500 buildings are empty and waiting to be filled with new ideas. To complete this task, the city invented its own administrative body, known as Kulturelle Stadtentwicklung (Cultural Urban Development), which is in charge of a process that attempts to move the city into a new era, as well as public space Mannheim grew as a city built for cars after the Second World War: broad streets, gigantic bridges, dark underpasses and elaborate parking guidance systems dominate its undeveloped urban space. Cycling in Mannheim is no fun. Progressive cities in Europe are slowly reducing their parking spaces, introducing cycle paths and improving public transport. What is Mannheim supposed to do with all these areas if cars are soon to disappear? A common solution is to turn urban constructions into parks, but there are enough green recreational areas here already. Mannheim is looking at a very eventful future.

And this is exactly where HOTEL shabbyshabby comes in. For the project is a revolution in urban development in small doses, disguised as a theatre festival programme. Little huts, erected like keyholes in the right places, open up new worlds – not only different views onto the beauty of the city, providing new angles on familiar things, but the view of a new future. A city that might function quite differently tomorrow, where public space is not just an area to cross on the way from A to B, but a site where the city is created and negotiated. We want the shabby hotels to be seen as prototypes for spaces where locals can give free rein to their imagination, in a way that everyone notices, giving others the courage to follow suit, and thus turn the city into a real metropolis and model city of everyday culture.

We'll be back!

HOTEL shabbyshabby
X Firmen
Die Schutzbefohlenen
Tararabumbia
Automobile
Riding on a cloud
Super Premium Soft Double Vanilla Rich
Kiste im Koffer
The Metastable Circuit 2
CRACKz
Dönüşüm Muhteşem Olacak! Change Will Be Terrific!
Sous leurs pieds, le paradis / Unter ihren Füßen, das Paradies
Ficção / Fiktion
Peaches Christ Superstar
The Conversationalist
You Are Not Alone
Next Day
Escuela / Schulung
Böse Geister
23. Mai
www.theaterderwelt.de
Mannheim 2014
08. Juni
CARO

Thyestes
Judith
Zoo
Bis zum Tod
Saddam Hussein –
A Mystery Play
Vortex Temporum
Turbulence
(a dance about the economy)
Macho Dancer
Partita 2
stepX Tanz für junges Publikum

shabbyshab
shabbyshab

DUS

258

TIME FLIGHT PANEL
BOOST IT!
OUTER LIGHTNING
FREE FLIGHT DEVICE
SOLAR CONTROL PANEL
SPEED CONTROL
IPHONE 6
OBSERVER
SONIC STABILIZER

e.lab

Weißglas

Living Room for the City

Fünf Girls aus Cambridge, die noch nie einen Akkuschrauber gesehen haben, sollen einen Turm bauen? Von Tag zu Tag sah man, wie sich ihre Fähigkeiten im Umgang mit Material, ihre Koordinationskompetenzen, Reaktionsfähigkeit und Teamgeist schärften. Als dann noch der Kran kam, waren Sie vollkommen aus dem Häuschen. Und das Ergebnis kann sich wirklich sehen lassen! Sowohl ästhetisch als auch an dieser exquisiten Lage am Neckar, direkt neben dem Musikpark.

Five girls from Cambridge who had never clapped eyes on a drill before they were supposed to build a tower? From day to day, their skills in dealing with materials, coordination, reacting to problems and team spirit grew visibly. When the crane finally arrived, they were completely beside themselves. And the results are visible, in terms of aesthetics and location, on an exquisite site on the Neckar, right beside the Musikpark.

Lukas Lendzinski

Whoofo

Die amerikanischen Truppen hinterließen Mannheim mit dem Benjamin Franklin Village eine vollkommen intakte Geisterstadt nach deutscher Wärmeschutzverordnung. Man könnte direkt einziehen – wären da nicht Architektur und Städtebau. Das Aufbrechen der Lagerarchitektur und der Umbau des Städtebaus, der eher an eine Schweinemastanlage erinnert, denn an ein Wohnviertel, wird der Stadt Mannheim außerirdische Kräfte abverlangen. Die ersten sind bereits da.

The American troops left the Benjamin Franklin Village behind in Mannheim – a fully intact ghost town that even fulfils German insulation regulations. It would be possible to move in straight away, if it wasn't for the architecture and urban planning. Breaking away from the warehouse-style architecture and converting the urban development evocative of a pig feeding plant more than a residential area, will require extra-terrestrial powers from the city of Mannheim. The first Martians have landed.

For'rest

Die gelungene Mischung aus Architektur und Gartengestaltung ist diesem polnischen Spezialistenteam gelungen. Die Pflanzen hatten eine besondere Herkunft: die USA! Denn sie kamen von dem ehemaligen US-Hoheitsgebiet des Benjamin Franklin Village. Wer nicht schon mit Heuschnupfen geplagt war, konnte das hier nachholen. Aber Erholung: die Nutzung des Wellnessbereichs des Dorint Hotels war inklusive.

This successful crossbreed of architecture and landscape planning was realised by a specialist Polish team. The plants came from the former US army territory of the Benjamin Franklin Village. Those who were not already suffering from hay fever could make up for lost time here. And as for restfulness, the Dorint Hotel's wellness area was included in the package.

Benjamin Foerster-Baldenius

Tubheim

Das lustigste Team! Sehr französisch, sie waren die ersten, die mit einem Bier in jeder Hand gearbeitet haben. Sie hatten keine Erfahrung mit Holz oder Elektrogeräten, aber sie haben es versucht und geschafft. Sie waren nicht sehr organisiert, aber immer fair und ehrlich. Ihre Regeln: keine Schrauben und nur recyceltes Material. Ihre Konstruktion war gut, denn sie war genau wie sie: flexibel, einfach und zerbrechlich. Trotz aller Schwierigkeiten waren sie sehr froh, an dem Projekt beteiligt zu sein, und einige hat es auch verändert: Sie wollen jetzt im Kollektiv bauen und architektonisch arbeiten!

The funniest team! Very French, they were the first people to work with a beer in either hand. They were not used to working with wood and power tools but they tried and they succeeded. They weren't very organised but fair and straight. Their rules: no screws and only recycled material. Their construction was good because it was like them: flexible, simple, and fragile. Despite all the difficulties, they were really happy to take part in this project and it even changed some of them: now they want to build and make architecture with people in a collective way!

Samuel Boche

Aufgev
in den

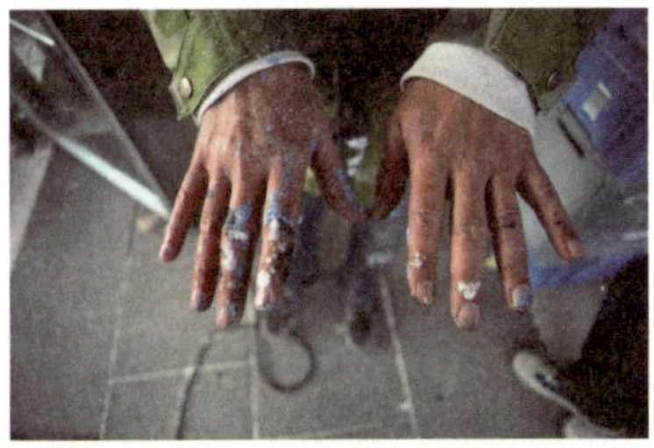

The Hedonist

Dieses Team war sehr darauf bedacht, dass der Raum auf Fotos gut aussah. Eine Person war für die Videoaufnahmen verantwortlich, was die Arbeitsweise des ganzen Teams beeinflusst hat.
Ich hatte zu diesem Team eine besondere Beziehung, weil der Organisator, Nuno, sich große Sorgen um die Konstruktion gemacht und jeden Abend mit mir darüber gesprochen hat. Das war gut, denn wenn man nicht auf der Baustelle ist, kann man einfach bei ein paar Bier reden!
Sie waren sehr froh über ihren Standort: die Neckarspitze, wo Neckar und Rhein ineinander fließen. Von dort hatte man einen wunderschönen Blick auf die BASF in Ludwigshafen.

This team was very focused on the fact that the room had to appear beautiful when photographed. One person was in charge of the video captions, which affected the way of working for the whole team. I had a special relationship with this team because the organiser, Nuno, was very worried about the construction itself and talked to me about these worries every evening. This was good because when you're not on the building site, you can talk easily over a few beers! They were very happy about the site: the Neckarspitze, where the Neckar and Rhine merge. There was a beautiful view onto BASF in Ludwigshafen.

Samuel Boche

Hotel Carl

Krach! Wieder ein Radler in das Hotelzimmer gecrasht... nun stand der Wagen mit dem Bett drin auch mitten auf dem Gehweg. Alles richtig SUPER! … Perfektes shabbyshabby-Hotel. Sehr sorgfältig gebaut und ausgedacht, eine fantastische Idee, die gegebenen Stadtmöbel zu benutzen. Nur gemein, dass die Lifaßsäule kein Balkon sein durfte! Dabei war das Schild so gut befestigt. Besonders schönes Detail: Dusche beim Kindergarten – einfach klingeln und die Kinder drehen den Wasserhahn auf.

Crash! Yet another cyclist crashes into the hotel room. Well, the car containing the hotel bed is standing in the middle of the pavement. Everything is wonderful, a perfect shabbyshabby hotel. Carefully built and constructed, a fantastic idea to use the existent city 'furniture'. But it was a pity that the ad column couldn't be turned into a balcony even though the sign was so well attached. An especially nice detail was the shower in the kindergarten; just ring the bell and the children would turn on the water.

Alexander Römer und David Moritz

Monumotel

Ein Hotelzimmer im Suite-Format mit großem Balkon und gediegener Parkanlage direkt vor der Haustür. Ein interdisziplinäres Team literaturbegeisterter Österreicher aus Bayern, wohnhaft in Berlin (oder so), basteln mit Hilfe der Mannheimer Freiwilligen Feuerwehr eine Hülle um den guten alten Friedrich Schiller, so dass ihm Hören und Sehen vergeht. Die Hotelbesucher kriegen hier zwar nix vorgelesen, können aber nachher von sich behaupten, einmal mit dem Meister eine Nacht verbracht zu haben.

A hotel room in the format of a suite with a large balcony and an elegant park right on the doorstep. An interdisciplinary team of Austrian enthusiasts for literature from Bavaria, who live in Berlin or thereabouts, built a cocoon around good old Friedrich Schiller with help from the Mannheim Volunteer Fire Department so that he could neither see, nor hear. The hotel guests were not read aloud to, but they could claim that they had spent the night with a master.

Peter Weigand

Fast Sleep Restaurant

Fastfood-Restaurants zu Wohnräumen umgebaut zu sehen, ist sicher ein noch nicht geträumter Traum der Slowfood-Gesellschaft. Ob man hier in der Nacht von Zombie-Burgern heimgesucht wurde oder ob einem der leibhaftige Ronald Mc Donald erschien, wissen wir leider nicht. Für die Hängekonstruktion wurden Schaukelhaken der unzähligen verwaisten Benjamin Franklin Village-Spielplätze verwendet. Die könnte die Stadt Mannheim einer Stadt schenken, in der es keine gibt, wie z.B. Paris, wo die Gruppe herkommt.

Converting fast food restaurants into apartments is certainly not a dream that comes from the slow food movement. Whether guests were plagued by zombie burgers at night, or if a lively Ronald McDonald appeared, we do not know. For the hanging construction, anchor hooks were used from the countless deserted playgrounds in the Benjamin Franklin Village. These were a gift from Mannheim to a place like Paris – where the group came from – that has none.

Benjamin Foerster-Baldenius

Draußen ist besser

Matthias Lilienthal
Künstlerischer Leiter des Festivals Theater der Welt 2014 in Mannheim, Intendant der Münchner Kammerspiele ab der Spielzeit 2015/16

Angefangen hat die Diskussion über das Projekt mit einem partizipatorischen Ansatz. Benjamin Foerster-Baldenius hatte von den Bellastock Festivals in Frankreich erzählt, bei denen 3000 Architekturstudenten in einem temporären Event Installationen aus einem vorgegebenen Material bauen. 3000 Menschen nach Mannheim einzuladen, traute ich mich nicht, dachte aber, dass bei 300 000 Einwohnern 1000 Studenten schon auffallen. Beim nächsten Treffen war die Frage, ob die Studenten nicht ein Thema brauchen und dadurch entstand die Idee, Hotelzimmer zu bauen: dezentrale Hotelräume im öffentlichen Raum. Dafür ist Mannheim ein gutes Pflaster, weil es in der Stadt Orte gibt, die man temporär zwischennutzen kann, dies aber nur selten gemacht wird. Auch beim ersten Blick auf das Nationaltheater fällt auf, dass es von großen freien Flächen umgeben ist.

Bei den Vorbereitungen eines Projekts ergeben sich dann pragmatische Veränderungen. Aus den 1000 Studenten werden 120, aus den 100 Zimmern werden 22. Sehr früh haben wir mit einer Befragung der Mannheimer Bevölkerung begonnen, an welchen Orten sie sich ein Hotelzimmer wünschen. Gefragt war besonders die zentrale Lage am Wasserturm, angekoppelt an idyllische Natur. Aber auch das Schillerdenkmal wurde früh genannt.

Das Projekt ergab eine Art ideelle Schnittstelle für das gesamte Festival. Mit internationalen Theaterfestivals wie Theater der Welt ist auch immer die Erwartungshaltung verbunden, dass exotische, unbekannte Welten vorgestellt werden. Dies drückt ja auch der Titel des Festivals aus, der vorgibt noch zu wissen, was die Welt ist und was Theater ist. Mann könnte es sich in der kuschligen Ecke von Welttheater bequem machen, aber auch schon das erste berühmt gewordene Festival 1981 in Köln hatte als zentrales Anliegen eine Werkschau von Pina Bausch aus dem nur 80 Kilometer entfernten Wuppertal.
Auch durch die Arbeit an dem Projekt „X Wohnungen" hatte ich immer wieder festgestellt, dass die eigentlich unbekannte Welt immer die Welt der eigenen Umgebung ist, während die touristische Welt zur vertrauten geworden ist. Die Hotelzimmer haben den Mannheimern und den Festivalbesuchern die Möglichkeit gegeben, einen fremden Blick auf die eigene Realität zu werfen. Die eingeladenen Inszenierungen bewegten sich auf der Höhe des internationalen Performancediskurs und verwehrten sich einer Reduzierung auf das kulturell Andere.

Etwa neun Monate vorher begannen wir, das Projekt mit einer internationalen Ausschreibung zu kommunizieren. Im Februar fand die öffentliche Vorstellung der Entwürfe und der ausgewählten Konzepte statt. So konnten wir früh auf das Projekt aufmerksam machen. 120 Studierende und Bastelwillige sind eine Woche vor Festivalstart angereist und haben in einer eigenen Zeltstadt und Werkstatt auf dem Platz vor dem Theater gelebt und gearbeitet. Auch über eine gemeinsame Küche entstand ein anderes Modell von Leben und es entwickelte sich so etwas wie ein Vorfestival.
Als dann schließlich die Zimmer an ihre Standorte gebracht wurden, gab es einen Walk durch die Stadt: 400 Menschen machten sich zu einem Rundgang auf, um die Zimmer zu sehen.

Über die ausgesuchten Plätze eroberte das Festival Orte in der Stadt, etwa die Neckarspitze, an der Neckar und Rhein zusammenfließen mit einem wunderbar urbanen Blick auf die BASF. Vielleicht der Ort, an dem man am besten Mannheim versteht: die Naturidylle der beiden Flüsse und der fast kitschige Blick auf ein Industriepanorama. Die Politik des

Oberbürgermeisters Dr. Peter Kurz konzentriert sich sehr darauf, dem Image des etwas heruntergekommenen ehemaligen Industriestandorts der Jahrtausendwende den Aufbau einer Creative City entgegenzustellen. Das Festival hat der Politik aber auch die Frage gestellt, ob sie dabei nicht die Mitnahme der industriellen Basis vergisst.

Die Befragung der Einwohner stellte klar, dass das Schillerdenkmal eine Art Brücke zwischen der kulturellen Identität und der temporären Architektur darstellt. Das Nationaltheater Mannheim steht wie ein großer Klotz in der Mitte der Stadt. Jeder Taxifahrer kennt es und es ist der klare Kristallisationspunkt der Stadt.
Schiller ist mit seiner Theaterarbeit in der Stadt der historische Bezugspunkt, mit dem auch klar das Schauspiel im Mittelpunkt steht. Burkhard C. Kosminski hat diesen Bezug in einen Ort für zeitgenössische Dramatik umformuliert, im kulturellen Gedächtnis spielt das Erbe aber nach wie vor eine große Rolle. Bei HOTEL shabbyshabby war das deutlich an der Begeisterung der Mannheimer für das Hotelzimmer, das das Schillerdenkmal überbaute, zu erkennen. In der Illustration des Entwurfs wurde Schillers steinerne Hand zum Handtuchhalter für die Hotelgäste. Das Verhältnis drehte sich spielerisch um. Normalerweise wird jeder Schüler Mannheims mit der „Glocke" gequält. Hier wird das Denkmal zum dienenden Gebrauchsgegenstand und der Mythos wird trivialisiert. Eine Nacht mit Schiller schlafen, auch nicht schlecht. Ich fand auch großartig, dass die Genehmigungsbehörden damit kein Problem hatten. Und die Übernachtenden hatten auch kein Problem damit, dass das Zimmer an heißen Tagen zu einer Sauna wurde.

Das Projekt thematisiert aber auch die für Deutschland wichtige Frage, wie Formen des Bauens gedacht werden können, die mit dem Provisorischen umgehen. Mit einem Budget von 250€ je Hotelzimmer plus Sachsponsoring ergab sich ein temporäres Bauen, das verschiedene Recyclingkonzepte ausprobierte.
Unter anderem entstand ein Dom, der die überall in der Bundesrepublik aussortierten Altglascontainer einer anderen Nutzung unterzog. Die kuppelförmigen Container wurden zu einer Miniaturausgabe der Hagia Sophia zusammengeschweißt. Aufgestellt wurde das Zimmer auf dem Marktplatz direkt vor den besten türkischen Restaurants der Stadt. Immer wieder klopften Neugierige an und wollten es besichtigen. Das war die Installation, die am meisten für Irritationen sorgte.
Die drei Zimmer auf dem Gelände des Benjamin Franklin Village stellten die Frage, wie die Stadt diese Kasernengelände zu einer heutigen Nutzung organisieren sollte: Eher in der Form einer langsamen Try and Error Nutzung, bei der temporäre Benutzer Hinweise auf Formen vernünftiger Nutzung geben. Das Verhältnis zwischen dem Gelände und der geplanten Nutzung ähnelt eher einem kürzlich gelandeten Ufo.

Immer wieder wurde von Mitgliedern des Freundesvereins des Nationaltheaters die Frage gestellt: Was haben Hotelzimmer mit Theater zu tun? Als erste Performer des Festivals waren die Bauteams zu sehen, die in weißen Maleranzügen in der open-air-Werkstatt vor dem Theater an den Zimmern arbeiteten.
Alle Übernachtenden waren eingeladen zu einem Hotelfrühstück in der Festivalkantine und dort tauschten sie mit den anderen Gästen die Erlebnisse der letzten Nacht aus. So erzählten sie sich gegenseitig ihre individuelle Theatervorstellung, in der allein die Perspektive auf die eigene Stadt, das Ausgesetztsein, aber auch der andere Blick auf die eigene Realität zum Thema wurde. Am vorletzten Tag des Festival erzählte eine Festivalbesucherin einer anderen, in welchen verschiedenen Zimmern sie geschlafen hatte und es wurde fast zu einem Wettbewerb, die eine in sechs, die andere in fünf. Die Frage, ob das jetzt Theater sei, wurde einfach übersprungen.

Outside is better

Matthias Lilienthal
Artistic Director of the Theater der Welt festival 2014 in Mannheim, and Director of the Münchner Kammerspiele from 2015/16

Discussions on this project began with a participatory approach. Benjamin Foerster-Baldenius told us about the Bellastock festival in France where 3,000 architecture students were invited to build installations from specified materials for a temporary event. I did not feel I could invite 3,000 people to Mannheim, but I thought that in a city where 300,000 people live, 1,000 students would also make their presence felt. At the next meeting, we discussed whether these students needed a theme. That was when the idea arose to construct non-central hotel rooms in public space. Mannheim is a good place to do this because there are plenty of sites that lend themselves to being used as temporary spaces, but this seldom happens. A cursory glance at the Nationaltheater revealed that it is surrounded by large areas of undeveloped land.

During the preparation for the project, some changes were made for pragmatic reasons: not 1,000 students, but 120, were invited, and not 100 rooms, but 22, were developed. At the very early stages, we carried out a survey among the residents of Mannheim asking where they wanted new hotel rooms to be located. The centre next to the water tower was especially popular, coupled with green spaces. But the Schiller memorial also came up early on.

The project became a kind of intersection of ideas for the entire festival. In the case of international theatre festivals like Theater der Welt, there is an expectation that exotic, foreign worlds will be presented. Even the festival's name claims to know what the world is, and what theatre is. One could snuggle down in the cosy corner of world theatre – but even the first festival, which gained renown in 1981 in Cologne, had the central aim of presenting a Pina Bausch retrospective from Wuppertal, 80 kilometres away.
And also while working on the "X Wohnungen" project, I kept coming up across the idea that the foreign world is the one we live in, whereas the tourist world has become familiar. The hotel rooms in Mannheim enabled people from the city and the festival visitors to look at their own reality from an unfamiliar perspective, while the productions invited worked on a level of international performance discourse that defied reduction to cultural 'otherness'.

About nine months prior to the festival's opening, we started to publicize the project with an international call for bids. In February there was a public presentation of the selected designs and concepts. This drew attention to the project early on. 120 students and eager craftspeople arrived in the city a week before the festival started, to live and work in a kind of tent city and workshop on the square in front of the theatre. Another kind of lifestyle grew out of the communal kitchen, and so, a kind of pre-festival developed. When the hotel rooms had been erected on their sites, there was a guided walk through the city in which 400 people took part.

With the various sites that were selected for HOTEL shabbyshabby, the festival was able to occupy parts of the city, such as the Neckarspitze, where the Neckar and Rhine run into one and where there is a marvellously urban view of the BASF factory. Perhaps this is the place where one can best understand the city: on one hand, the natural idyll of the two rivers, and on the other, the almost kitschy industrial panorama. The policies of Mannheim's mayor, Dr. Peter Kurz, are very focused on revamping the image of this former base of industry from the turn of the millennium, now somewhat rundown, and replacing it with one of a creative city. But the festival also posed the question as to whether this approach has omitted to incorporate Mannheim's industrial roots.

The residents' questionnaire made it clear that the Schiller memorial acts as a kind of bridge between cultural identity and temporary architecture. The Nationaltheater sticks out like a huge blot on the landscape in the city centre. Every taxi driver knows it, and it is clearly the city's main landmark.
Schiller, with his theatrical work, is the city's historical point of reference; at its core is obviously the stage. Burkhard C. Kosminski has reworded this reference, and has called Mannheim a site of contemporary drama; but in cultural memory, Schiller's legacy still plays a major role. In the HOTEL shabbyshabby project this was palpable in the enthusiasm shown by the locals for the hotel room that was built around the Schiller memorial. In the design drawings, Schiller's stone hand was turned into a towel hook for guests. The relationship was turned around in a playful way: normally every Mannheim schoolchild is coerced into reading Glocke (The Song of the Bell). Here the memorial is turned into an object to serve the public, and the myth becomes trivialised. Spending a night with Schiller: not bad. I was also delighted that the authorities didn't see this as a problem. And the guests staying the night didn't see it as a problem that the room turned into a sauna on hot days.

The HOTEL shabbyshabby project also raises issues that are important for the whole of Germany, such as how forms of construction can be conceived that deal with provisional projects. For a budget of 250 € per hotel room plus product sponsoring, a temporary building was produced that tried out different recycling concepts.
Among others, a dome construction was built using transformed glass recycling containers – of the type that you see everywhere in Germany. The cupola-shaped containers were soldered together into a miniature version of the Hagia Sophia. The room was erected on the market square, right in front of the best Turkish restaurants in town. Curious passers-by constantly knocked at the door and wanted to look inside. It was the installation that caused the most puzzlement.
The three rooms on the grounds of the Benjamin Franklin Village posed the question as to how the city should reallocate these former barracks a new purpose – in the form of a slow try-and-error usage, in which temporary users give tips on workable forms of utilization. The relationship between the grounds and the planned use was more akin to a recently landed UFO.

Time and again, members of the Friends' Association of the Nationaltheater asked what the hotel rooms had to do with theatre. The construction workers were among the first performers of the festival, working on their rooms in white overalls in the open-air workshop in front of the theatre.
All overnight guests were invited to a hotel breakfast in the festival canteen, where they swapped stories with other guests about their stay. So there was an exchange of individual 'theatre performances', in which the perspective of one's own town, and being exposed to another view of one's own reality, was under discussion. On the penultimate day of the festival, one visitor told another how many of the rooms she had slept in, and it almost turned into a contest – the one had slept in five, the other in six. They simply skipped the question of whether or not it was theatre.

EUROPLANT
EUROPLANT
BIO
EUROPLANT

SCHE
BETT
MACH MICH AN!
CARL

BETT

shabbyshabby für alle

Lukasz Lendzinski
Studio umschichten, Stuttgart

Eine schöne Idee wird Realität. Aber wie geht es jetzt weiter? Was können wir von so einem Projekt lernen? Was sagt so ein Projekt über eine Stadt aus? Soll es mehr von diesen Projekten geben und warum? Warum dürfen die Dinge nicht so bleiben, wie in diesen Festival-Tagen? Warum müssen wir wieder in den grauen Alltag zurückkehren? Es war doch real…

Ein gelungenes Projekt, würde man sagen.

Was ist ein gelungenes Projekt? Und für wen? Für Hotelbesucher, für die Hotelerbauer, für die Anwohner, das Theater, die Mannheimer?

Zwar haben sich die Besucher der Hotels über das eine oder andere tropfende Dach gefreut und haben die eine oder andere sonderbare, schöne, neue Aussicht genossen, zu der sie sonst keinen Zugang gehabt hätten. Und die Erbauer haben sich gefreut, dass sie so jung nun schon eine echte Architektur erbauen durften.

Aber warum ist das nur ein Ausnahmezustand? Ist unserer ganzes Leben nicht ein Ausnahmezustand? Für die einen mag es ein weiteres schönes Projekt in der Stadt sein, für die anderen ist es ein Teil ihrer Arbeits- und somit Lebenszeit.

HOTEL shabbyshabby hat gezeigt, wie viel Energie und wie viel Gemeinschaft möglich ist, wenn man für eine Sekunde im Leben von Mannheim einen Ausnahmezustand zulässt: rund 150 Menschen wuseln in einem Camp herum, das an einer lauten Kreuzung am Theater steht. Da kommt Chloé um die Ecke und hat in der linken Hand den Mixer mit den noch tropfenden Himbeeren und in der rechten den gerade von den Bauteams meist gesuchten und scheinbar einzigen 25mm-Topfbohrer. In einer ausbalancierten Wortjonglage aus Deutsch, Englisch und Französisch vermittelt sie den Bohrer an die Multikulti-Bauteams. Gleichzeitig stößt Paula am Handy einen Freudenschrei aus und bestätigt die Zusage von mehreren Baubohlen der Großbaustelle gegenüber, die wir spontan noch für das Projekt der Britischen Girls brauchen. Nicht zu verachten – die telefonische Grundlage für diese Verhandlung, die unsere Geheimwaffe, der lokale Super-Statiker Joachim Pachmann, gelegt hat. Dann wäre da noch Arno, der zwischen einer weit in die Zukunft reichenden Planung und einer notwendigen sofortigen Handlungsreaktion die Balance schafft. Celine, die die letzten Spezialmaterialien aus den Kellern ihrer Mannheimer Freunde organisiert und – naturalnie – Mama Marta.

All dies in einem Rahmen, der dafür ja auch erst geschaffen werden musste. Das Festival Theater der Welt mit Matthias als Flaggschiff und einem Team, das an das

Unmögliche glaubt. Benni von raumlabor, der mit seiner guten Nase ernste Themen der Stadtentwicklung aufspürt und zeigt, wie wir zukünftige Herausforderungen mit einer Leichtigkeit angehen können, die jeder Bürger versteht. Er kennt die Notwendigkeit einer guten Zusammenstellung eines perfekten Teams, das in der Lage ist, auf eine sich ständig verändernde Umgebung immer die richtige Lösung anzubieten. Nicht zuletzt sei da auch die Stadt Mannheim erwähnt, die bestimmt über den einen oder anderen Schatten springen musste, um die Qualität eines solchen innovativen Formates zu erkennen und zuzulassen. Das muss man sich erstmal trauen.

Für ein gutes Projekt-Setting ist außerdem leckeres Essen absolut notwendig. Dreimal am Tag haben Kira und Marius uns mit scheinbar unendlichen Variationen der veganen Küche gute Laune beschert. Dass es sonst immer so schwer scheint, in Kantinen lecker zu kochen, kann nur an den strengen Sicherheitsbestimmung liegen. Abgerundet wurden diese wundervollen Tage durch die überbesetze Bar, dessen Team sich nichts leichteres zu Ziel setzte, als die Meute mit frisch pürierten Erdbeer-Daiquiris und anderen Spineranzien glücklich zu machen, die einem so am Tag einfallen, wenn man nichts anderes machen muss, als Cocktailkataloge zu wälzen.

Also zusammengefasst:
Wir leben dort, wo wir arbeiten, wir essen dort, wo wir schlafen. Wir machen Party zusammen und weinen zusammen. Wir wachen zusammen auf und bauen was in die Stadt hinein. Klingt doch ein wenig nach aktuellen großen städtebaulichen Richtlinien, wo uns das Zusammenführen von „Arbeiten und Wohnen" zu horrenden Preisen schmackhaft gemacht wird. Wir haben zwar nicht so viel Geld wie diese Großprojekte (man bedenke, dass eine Hütte nur 250€ Budget hatte), aber wir machen mehr als das Beste daraus. Und am Ende ist keiner sauer, wenn eine Fuge nicht ganz akkurat ist oder wenn an der einen oder anderen Stelle ein Eimer unter der tropfenden Decke steht.
So ein Vorgehen hinterfragt unsere aktuelle Baukultur. Wenn wir ansonsten von Hotelprojekten oder anderen großen Projekten in Städten hören, dann denken wir doch eigentlich immer nur an Kostensprengungen, Anwälte, Ärger mit Bürgern und sich scheinbar bis ins unendliche verschiebende Eröffnungsversprechen.

Ein Plädoyer für die Unperfektheit.
Hier stehen das gemeinschaftliche Bauen und das Gebäude im Vordergrund und nicht die Regressansprüche. Die Möglichkeiten, die wir haben, müssen uns reichen – alles ist so, wie es ist. Der Motor ist die Übergabe an und die Übernahme von Verantwortung durch alle Mitspieler und Beteiligten. Jeder ist für sein Tun verantwortlich und das mobilisiert und schafft Vertrauen. Darauf basieren unsere Gemeinschaft und unsere Städte. Ich frage mich, wie das wohl aussieht, wenn wir mal ein ganzes Viertel oder die Kasernenflächen bearbeiten sollen...?

shabbyshabby for everyone

Lukasz Lendzinski
Studio umschichten, Stuttgart

A beautiful idea becomes reality. But what happens now? What can we learn from a project like this? What does this project say about a city? Should there be more projects like these – and why? Why can't things stay the way they were during the festival? Why do we have to go back a to boring, humdrum routine?
But it was all real…
A success, you could say.
What is a successful project? And for whom? For hotel guests, for the hotel constructors, for residents, the theatre, the people of Mannheim?
It's true that the guests in these hotels were happy to spend the night under the occasional leaking roof and were able to enjoy the occasionally peculiar, beautiful or new view like no other. And the architecture students were happy to be given the opportunity to build a real construction so early on in their careers.
But why is this all an exception to the norm? Aren't our lives exceptions to the norm?
For some, it might just have been another nice project; for others, part of his or her working time, which also means lifetime.

HOTEL shabbyshabby showed how much energy and community is possible if, for a second, life in Mannheim is allowed to become an exception from the norm: about 150 people bustled about in a camp, which stood on a noisy crossroads by the theatre. A scene: Chloé comes around the corner, a mixer in her hand that is still dripping with raspberries, and in her right, the most sought-after, perhaps only, 25 mm drill. Using a potpourri of language, equal parts English, German and French, she hands the drill over to the multicultural construction team. Meanwhile, Paula lets out a shriek of joy while on her mobile phone because the construction site opposite has confirmed their pledge of several planks that we suddenly need for the British girls' project. And not to be scoffed at – the basis for this telephone negotiation was laid by Joachim Pachmann, our secret weapon and local engineer extraordinaire. Then there's Arno, who manages to create a balance between far-reaching future planning and the necessary instant action response. And Celine, who organised the last-minute special requests for materials by rooting through her friends' Mannheim cellars. And – naturalnie – there is Mama Marta.

All this took place within a frame that first had to be created: the Theater der Welt festival with Matthias at the mast and his team who believed in the impossible. And Benni from raumlabor, who has a good nose for key issues in urban development and who showed us ways in which we can approach challenges in the future with a lightness that every layperson can grasp. He understands how essential it is to put together the perfect team; one that is capable of offering the right solution in a constantly changing environment. And last but not least, there was the city of Mannheim that had to swallow its pride on occasion in order to acknowledge and support such an innovative format. That takes some guts.

A good setting for a project also requires delicious food. Three times a day, Kira and Marius served us with apparently never-ending variations of vegan cuisine. Because it always seems impossible to frin delicious food in a canteen, I can only think it has something to do with safety regulations. These wonderful days were rounded off at the crowded bar, whose team didn't have a simple task in serving the gang with freshly puréed strawberry daiquiris and other fripperies that you can only come up with when you have nothing to do all day except pore over cocktail books.

So, in summary: we lived where we worked, and ate where we slept. We partied together and we cried together. We woke up together and built something into the cityscape. It sounds a little like those modern city development guidelines, in which a fusion of 'Life' and 'Work' is sold to us for horrendous prices. We may not have had as much money as these major planning projects (per hut the maximum budget was 250 €), but we made the most of it. And in the end, no one was angry if a joint wasn't perfect, or if here and there, a bucket had to catch raindrops leaking through the roof.
This approach poses questions about our culture of construction. If we hear about hotel projects or other large-scale projects elsewhere, we associate them with exploding costs, lawyers, trouble with residents and promises of inaugurations that are endlessly postponed.

A plea for imperfection.
At the foreground is a collaborative construction approach, and the building itself – not compensation claims; the possibilities we have; things being are as they are. The driving force is the handing over and acceptance of responsibility by all parties and participants. Each person is responsible for his or her actions, and this mobilises and creates trust. That is what our communities are based on, and our cities too. I wonder how it would look if we were allowed to reconstruct an entire district such as grounds of barracks or on the barrack grounds…?

UMBAU
RÄUMUNGS
VERKAUF
MARKENMODE REDUZIERT
AB 5. JUNI 2014
engelhorn
ONE WAY

Douglas

WERKHAUS
NTM
WERKHAUS
NTM

ZORN

Collini Bay Resort

Die Mannheimer Lokalmatadore wissen einfach, was ihrer Stadt noch fehlt: ein amtlicher Partybeach mit Übernachtungsmöglichkeit. Egal, was die Wasserqualität sagt und wie das Wetter so ist, die drei Architekten machen schon mal den Anfang mit einer kleinen Hotel-Anlage im Paletten-Style direkt am Collini Steg im Neckar-Hochwasser-Überflutungsbereich.

The local matadors from Mannheim simply knew what their hometown was missing: a state-approved party beach with overnight quarters. The water quality was not important, and neither was the weather – these three architects took the first steps towards their goal with a little pallet-style hotel right by the Collini Bridge in the Neckar flood area.

Peter Weigand

Zum Goldenen Flaschenzug

Sich selbst aus dem einen Universum in das andere zu ziehen ist, ein Kraftakt mit langer Kette (220 m). Außerdem schwingt es, je nach Windstärke, mehr oder weniger bedrohlich da oben. Wieder auf dem Boden am nächsten Morgen, gibt es dieses Phänomen von Landkrankheit, durch die nächtliche Anpassung an das Luftige fällt der Start in den Tag noch ein bisschen schwerer als sonst. Allerdings tut der erfrischende Sprung in den Ententeich noch vor Öffnung des Parks ganz gut. Regnen sollte es nicht unbedingt, da nicht viel Platz auf der Plattform für eine geräumige wasserdichte Zeltstruktur ist.

To pull yourself from one universe to another requires strength and a long chain of 220 metres. Besides this, the wind swings you from side to side to the top. Once back on the ground, you feel a kind of land sickness: by adjusting to the airiness up there, the start of the day feels more heavy than usual. But the refreshing dip in the duckpond before the park opens does you a world of good.

Alexander Römer und David Moritz

StattTheater

Das Versteck im Bauzaun – spitze! Die einseitig spiegelnde Folie war das wichtigste Element und gleichzeitig der größte Unsicherheitsfaktor. Hat aber dann ganz hervorragend geklappt. Spitzenmäßig! Schön inszeniert: der großzügige Ausblick auf die Straße und das Schlafen auf Beinhöhe der Passanten – die Matratze konnte nach Wahl entweder nahtlos an die spiegelnde Scheibe oder ein paar Sicherheitszentimeter nach hinten gerückt werden. Der Raum zurückhaltend in schwarzem Molton gekleidet, einzig ein streifendes Oberlicht der Straßenlaterne bei Nacht.

The hiding place in the construction site fence – wonderful! The one-way reflective foil was the most important element as well as the biggest insecurity factor. But in the end, it worked very well. Absolutely wonderful in fact! Nicely executed: there was a generous view onto the street and you slept at eye level with legs of passers-by whereby the mattress could be placed immediately next to the reflective surface, or moved back a few centimetres to safety. The only light was that of the streetlamp overhead as the room was kitted out entirely in black molton.

Alexander Römer und David Moritz

Stadtloge

Das Team war sehr gut organisiert, man hatte das Gefühl, mit einer Gruppe alter Freunde zusammenzuarbeiten. Drei hatten Werkzeug und wussten, wie man mit Holz umgeht, daher waren sie als Team unabhängig. Die Nähe des Standorts war ebenfalls von Vorteil für sie. Ich war nur beim schwierigsten Bauabschnitt dabei. Sie trafen nie eine wichtige Entscheidung ohne mich, hatten einen festgelegten Arbeitsplan und riefen mich immer an, um den nächsten Tag abzusprechen. Ihr Raum gehört zu meinen Favoriten. Eine schöne Konstruktion, ein Erfolg.

They were very well organised, and it was like working together with an old group of friends. Three of them had tools and knew how to work with wood, so they were independent as a team. The proximity of the site was another advantage for them. I was only with them for the difficult parts of the construction. They never made an important decision without me, they had a defined schedule and always called me the day before to organise the day. I think their room is one of my favourites. Nice construction, a success.

Samuel Boche

Der Standort auf dem Dach des Werkhauses vom Nationaltheater war exklusiv und passte natürlich erstklassig zum Namen. Schlüssigerweise wurde auch das gesamte Zimmer aus wiederverwendeten Bühnenbildern und fast ohne Baukosten errichtet.

The location on the roof of the Nationaltheater Werkhaus was exclusive and was of course very apt for the chosen name of this hotel. Logically, all the rooms were made of recycled set designs and with almost no construction costs.

Benjamin Foerster-Baldenius

JCDecaux

Grünglas
Grünglas
Weißglas

kenversicherung

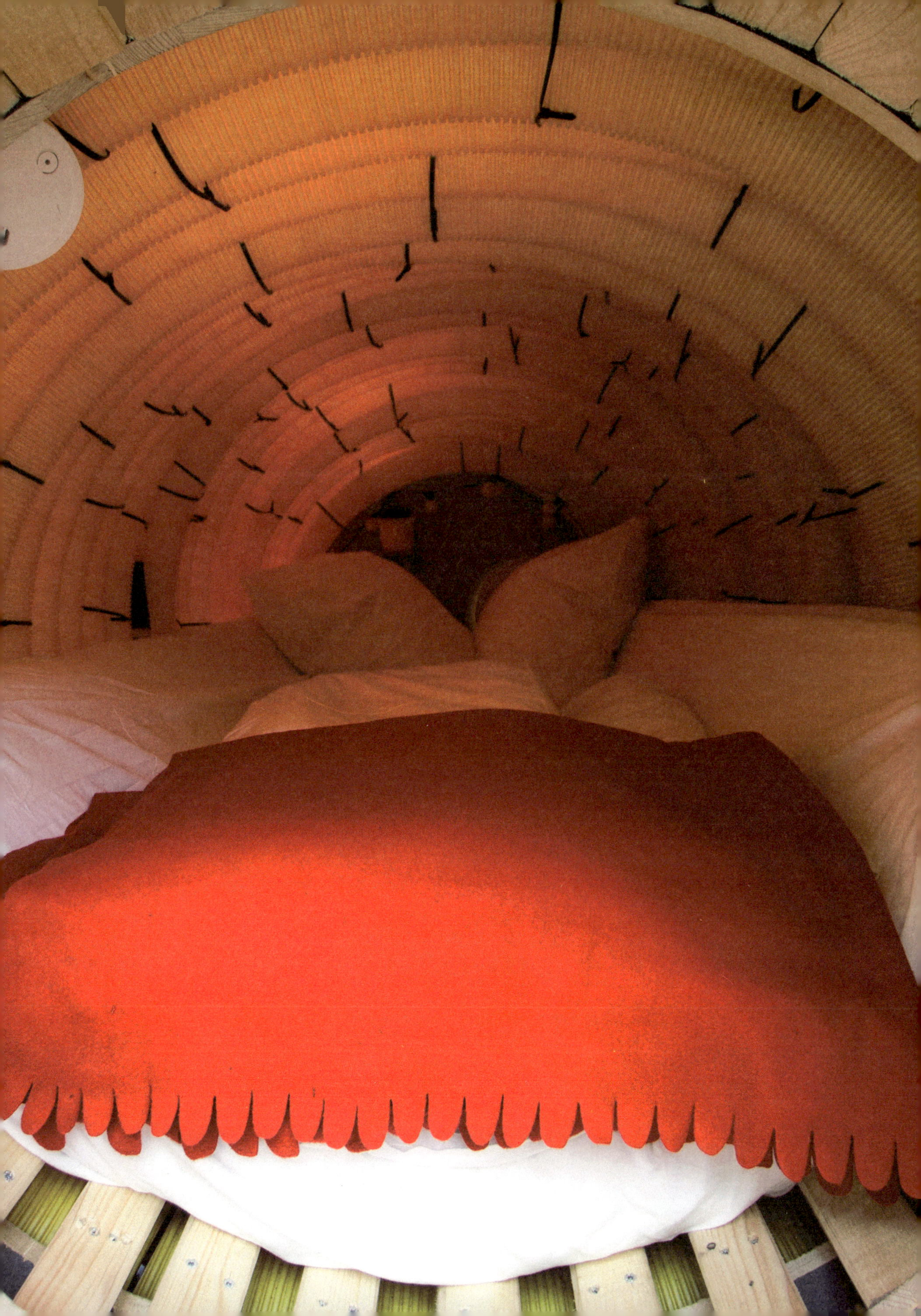

TECHNOSEUM
MÜLLERS

Prinz Käse

Ein Cocon aus Dränage-Rohren konstruiert von zwei Mädels. Was anderenortes als verkrampfte Frauenquote versucht wird zu etablieren, passiert hier einfach. Frauen an der Säge, Frauen auf dem Gerüst, Frauen konstruieren, Frauen bauen. Frauen sind toll.

A cocoon made of drainpipes constructed by two women. Whereas elsewhere, uptight attempts at establishing women's representation are made, this just happened here, all by itself. Women sawing, on the scaffolding, building: women are wonderful.

Lukas Lendzinski

Der Standort unseres kleinsten Hotelzimmers wäre noch zu erwähnen: G7 ist das größte der Mannheimer Quadrate (und ist eigentlich ein Rechteck), in der Mitte gibt es eine interne Erschließungsstraße, an der liegt nicht nur das Theater TiG7 sondern auch der ruhigste Kreisverkehr der Stadt.

The site of our smallest hotel room should also be mentioned. G7 is the biggest of all Mannheim's grids (and it is in fact a rectangle); in the centre there is an internal access road on which lies not only the TiG7 theatre but also the quietest roundabout in the city.

Benjamin Foerster-Baldenius

3-Lichter-Hotel

(Gefühlt) 10 lustige Franzosen in Mannheim: Ausgangspunkt ist die (Straßenlaternen-)Nachttischlampe, die schon da steht – drum herum wird nur noch ein Haus gebaut. Was aussieht wie eine Mischung aus Gewächshaus und das vom Nikolaus, ist in Wahrheit ein Hotelzimmer im Minimal-Design der Sperrholzgeneration. Über ein ausgeklügeltes Seilzugsystem öffnet sich ein Kläppchen und man steht in einem hellen Raum mit Rundum-Blick auf den Neckar.

What felt like 10 funny Frenchmen in Mannheim: the starting point was the (streetlamp) nightlight that was already there – and around it, a hotel room was built. What looked like a cross between a greenhouse and the 'House of Santa Claus' was in fact a minimally designed hotel room by the plywood generation. Via an ingenuous winch-pull system, a little trapdoor opened up and you found yourself standing in a bright room with a panoramic view of the Neckar.

Peter Weigand

Da man, sobald es dunkel wird, ebenso von „rundum" gesehen werden kann, wurde den Passanten mit charmant französischem Akzent erklärt, dass es sich bei dem exponierten Raum um ein privates Bordell handele. Die verhaltene Begeisterung der Mannheimer hat die Franzosen letztendlich dazu bewegt, noch einen Tisch und zwei Stühle, die nach Wahl über die drei leuchtenden Kugeln gestülpt werden konnten, zu entwerfen.

Once it is dark out you can be seen from all sides. Men with charming french accents tell passerby that it is a private brother. The restrained enthusiasm this was met with from locals caused the French team to add the design of a table and two chairs that could be placed over the three shining streetlamps.

Paula Strunden

Schlafdom

Das professionellste Team! Sie brachten eigenes Werkzeug und eine Menge Erfahrung mit. Sie waren gut organisiert und planten alles durch, blieben aber offen für bauliche Veränderungen. Für mein Empfinden bestand dieses Team aus Künstlern, nicht Architekten. Sie sprachen über Farben, Formen, Volumen und ihre Beziehung zur Öffentlichkeit. Sie waren am richtigen Ort – auf dem Marktplatz – und immer bereit, mit der Öffentlichkeit über ihr Projekt zu sprechen.

The most professional team! They brought their own tools and experience. Well organised, they planned everything but were very open to adapting their construction. I felt that this team were artists, not architects. They spoke about colours, shapes, volumes and their relationship to the public. They were in the right place – the market square – always open to speaking about their project to the public on the street.

Samuel Boche

Nicht zu vergessen: Es handelt sich hier um ein Entwurfskonzept mit Zukunft: in Deutschland werden bald tausende Altglascontainer entsorgt! Die Gruppe hat hiermit einen Prototyp für Hotelzimmer, Kioske, Mini-Moscheen, Fahrradgaragen etc., etc. aus recycelten Altglas-Iglus präsentiert.

No small detail: This is a design concept with a future. In Germany, thousands of glass recycling containers will soon be disposed of! With their design, the group has constructed a prototype for hotel rooms, kiosks, mini-mosques, bicycle garages and so on.

Benjamin Foerster-Baldenius

shabbyshabby

Die Bauprobe

Heike Schuppelius
Professorin für Szenografie,
Hochschule für Gestaltung,
Karlsruhe

Wer hat sich nicht schon einmal gefragt, wie es wäre, in der eigenen Stadt zu Gast zu sein, als Tourist durch die Straßen zu gehen und den Blick eines Fremden einzunehmen? Wie würde sich der Blick auf die Stadt und die persönlichen Orte verändern, wenn man nicht in den gewohnten vier Wänden übernachtet, sondern in einem Hotelzimmer erwacht und sich, fernab von den alltäglich bekannten Wegen, die Stadt aus einer anderen Perspektive neu erschließt? Die Möglichkeit dies zu tun steht jedem frei und ist vielleicht sogar empfehlenswert, vorausgesetzt man kann und möchte sich das leisten.

In Mannheim aber hatte dieser Gedanke mit HOTEL shabbyshabby eine weitere Dimension. Die 22 über die Stadt verteilten, temporären Übernachtungsmöglichkeiten gestalteten sich in ihrer Ortswahl und Gestalt so spektakulär und unterschiedlich, wie ihre Autoren selbst; man hätte sie fast alle ausprobieren mögen.

Der Stadtraum Mannheims glich einem großen Experimentierfeld, in dem zwanzig Künstler- und Architektenteams sich und ihre Ideen ausprobieren konnten, in dem Studierende und Berufsanfänger die Gelegenheit bekamen, ihre Entwürfe im Maßstab 1:1 umzusetzen und gleichzeitig bereits die Aufmerksamkeit einer großen Öffentlichkeit genossen.

Im Kontext Theater wäre das in etwa vergleichbar mit der dort üblichen „Bauprobe". An diesem Tag, der bereits mit Produktionsbeginn feststeht, wird der Entwurf des Bühnenbildes mit möglichst einfachen und kostengünstigen Materialien am Originalort simuliert, um die Dimensionen, Proportionen und Eigenheiten des Raumkonzeptes zu überprüfen, bevor es in den Werkstätten umgesetzt wird. Es ist der Tag, an dem die Ideensammlung und Konzeption im Modell zu Ende gebracht und im Originalmaßstab auf Realisierbarkeit überprüft wird. In der Regel sind Bühnenbildner, Regisseur, Kostümbildner, Darsteller und Werkstattleiter anwesend, um sich selbst ihr Bild des geplanten Raumvorhabens zu machen, es zu überdenken und Korrekturen vorzunehmen. Es ist ein besonderes Erlebnis und manche Bauproben waren für mich schöner, spielerischer und experimenteller als das spätere Ergebnis. Das besondere aber ist der Schritt in den Originalmaßstab, die unmittelbare Erfahrung, die Idee umzusetzen, die bisher nur virtuell im Kopf und 3-dimensionaler Darstellung in Miniatur gereift ist. In dieser Hinsicht war HOTEL shabbyshabby eine ideale Ergänzung und Fortführung der Lehre an den Hochschulen und Universitäten, an denen es nicht oft die Möglichkeit gibt, sich über die Größe eines Möbelstückes hinaus im doch notwendigen Maßstab 1:1 zu erproben. Ein Stadtraumprojekt wie HOTEL shabbyshabby erzeugt in diesem Kontext Synergien zwischen Lehre und angewandter Praxis, die nur selten zu finden, geschweige denn zu realisieren sind.

„Hallo Welt“ lautete einer der Festivalslogans auf den Umhängetaschen und Plakaten, die im ganzen Stadtraum präsent waren. Ein internationales Theaterfestival zu Gast in Mannheim, das sich zudem nicht ausschließlich hinter verschlossenen Theatertüren präsentierte, sondern mit verschiedenen Formaten hinaus drängte in den öffentlichen Raum. Eingeläutet wurde die Bespielung des Stadtraumes aber schon vor dem offiziellen Festivalstart, mit dem Bezug des Festivalzentrums, das gleichzeitig den über hundert Architekten und Designern der temporären Hotelzimmer als Werkstatt, Übernachtungsmöglichkeit, Kantine und Treffpunkt diente und zum Herz des Festivals wurde. Nach getaner Arbeit wurden hier die letzten bauamtlichen Auflagen der Stadt entgegengenommen, wurde gemeinsam gegessen, diskutiert und der offene Arbeitsprozess fortgeführt. Während des Festivals konnte man hier morgens auf der Frühstücksterrasse zahlreiche Hotelgäste antreffen, die übernächtigt oder hellwach ihre Übernachtungserlebnisse austauschten.
Das Stadtraumprojekt HOTEL shabbyshabby hat die Neugier der Mannheimer für ihre eigene Stadt geweckt. Dass eine Übernachtung in einem der 22 Hotelzimmer für die Festivalbesucher ein einmaliges Erlebnis war, ist sicher. Ein besonderes und bleibendes Ereignis aber muss es für die Mannheimer gewesen sein, ihre Stadt auf diese Weise neu zu entdecken.

The Set Design Mock-up

Heike Schuppelius
Professor for Scenography,
Hochschule für Gestaltung
(Academy of Design),
Karlsruhe

Who hasn't paused to think how it would feel to be a guest in your own city – to walk through the streets as a tourist, and be seen as a stranger? How would your view of the city and your favourite spots change if you didn't sleep within your own four walls, but in a hotel far away from familiar routines – giving you a new way of looking at your town? It's an opportunity that everyone can take up. And, provided that you can and want to pay for it, it's to be recommended.

But for the HOTEL shabbyshabby project in Mannheim, this idea took on an extra dimension. The 22 temporary hotel rooms dotted across the city were planned in ways that were just as spectacular and distinctive in terms of location and design as their creators; one would have liked to try them all out.

Mannheim's urban space was turned into a space of experimentation, in which 20 teams of artists and architects were given the freedom to try out their ideas, and in which students and career entrants had the opportunity to build their designs as full-scale models in front of a large-scale audience.
In a theatre context, this process is comparable to the customary "set design mock-up": fixed at the beginning of a production, on which the set design is built in simulated form using the simplest, most inexpensive materials possible. This enables the team to check the dimensions, proportions and peculiarities of the spatial concept before putting it into practice in the workshop. It's the day when brainstorming and conception come together in a model, and the set size is checked for feasibility. Set designers, directors, costume designers, actors and workshop managers are present to get an idea of the planned space, think it through and make corrections. It is a unique experience, and has resulted in some set designs that were more beautiful, playful and experimental than the real thing.

But the special quality of the set design mock-up is the real-life experience of putting an idea into practice as a full-scale model – a virtual idea, up until this point, which has matured as a 3D miniature form. Seen this way, HOTEL shabbyshabby was the ideal counterpart to and continuation of teaching practices in universities and colleges: here, the experience of testing out one's capacities by building full-scale models is often lacking for anything bigger than a piece of furniture. In this context, an urban space project like HOTEL shabbyshabby creates synergies between teaching and practice that are rarely found, let alone implemented.

"Hello World" was one of the festival's slogans, appearing on tote bags and posters all over the city: this was an international theatre festival that did not present itself exclusively behind closed theatre doors, but also forced its way into Mannheim's public space in various formats. But use of public space as theatre space began even before the festival officially started with the occupation of the festival centre, which was turned into a workshop, hotel, canteen and meeting point by over a hundred architects and designers, and which became the festival's heart. Once the work was completed, this is where the city's final construction requirements were received, where joint dinners and discussions took place, and the working process continued. During the festival, many guests – either wide awake or tired out – could be found recounting their tales of overnight stays during breakfast on the tarrace of the festival centre.

In many cases, the HOTEL shabbyshabby project awakened the curiosity of local residents in their own city. And while it was quite an experience for festival visitors to spend the night in one of the 22 hotel rooms, it was certainly a special and lasting experience for the locals of Mannheim to discover their city in this entirely new way.

20
19
16

Mama Peter Löres

Warum sollte ein umgestürzter Hochsitz, der auf einen Kunstverein neben einer Hauptstraße gefallen ist, ein Hotelzimmer werden? Warum nicht, kann man hier nur drauf antworten.

Why should a toppled tower that has fallen onto an art gallery next to a main road be turned into a hotel room? The answer can only be: why not?

Lukas Lendzinski

Das Material waren die Überreste einer Aktion zu Sprengungen, die die Karlsruher Szenografiestudenten ein Jahr zuvor an der heute abgerissenen Mannheimer Kunsthalle gemacht haben. Das Zimmer sollte ursprünglich auch dort entstehen, was aber nicht mehr möglich war. Der Kunstverein, als ein Relikt aus der gleichen architektonischen Periode, war eine passende Alternative.

The material consisted of the remains of a project about explosions carried out by Karlsruhe set design students a year previously at the Mannheim Kunsthalle, now torn down. The room was previously supposed to be erected on that spot but this was no longer possible. The art gallery was a fitting alternative – a relic from the same architectural period.

Benjamin Foerster-Baldenius

Under my Umbrella

Anfangs viel reden und (um-)planen mit wenig Baufortschritt, aber auf der Hälfte der Zeit wurde dann Gas gegeben :-) … yeah, yeah! … und dann waren da plötzlich 200 bunte Regenschirme aufgespannt (alle liegen geblieben beim Mannheimer Einzelhandel) … eine wilde Blubberblase, die am Bug des Museumsschiffes hängengeblieben ist. Schöne Ausblick-Schnipsel zwischen den Schirmen mit Regenschutz und Minibar. Super, wenn am Schluss selbst für solche Details noch Zeit ist!

At the beginning there was a lot of discussion with little progress in construction, but halfway through, they stepped on the gas and…bingo! Suddenly 200 coloured umbrellas were put up (all left behind in Mannheim stores) like a froth of bubbles at the prow of the boat. A beautiful view in between the umbrellas, with protection from the rain and a mini-bar. How wonderful when there's still time left to include details like this!

Alexander Römer und David Moritz

Fairy Tank

Franzosen machens einfach nicht ohne Pool. In einer minimalen Konstruktion wird in einem der schönsten Parks von Mannheim eine kleine Kapsel auf eine Fontäne gesetzt und von ein paar fliegenden Schirmen verziert. Neben so profanen Problemen wie Dichtung und Abschließbarkeit entfaltet sich der Charme dieses Hotelzimmers vor allem in den Abendstunden, wenn die Besucher den Park verlassen haben und sich die Elfen vorsichtig aus ihren Verstecken trauen – auf einen kleinen Plausch am hotelzimmer-eigenen Pool mit den Glühwürmchen – und die Gesänge der Seerosenprinzessinnen von nebenan erklingen.

The French simply don't do it without a pool. In a minimalist construction, in one of the most beautiful parks in Mannheim, a little capsule was placed on a fountain and decorated with a few umbrellas. Besides the mundane problems of how to seal and lock the room, the charm of this hotel room unfolded in the evening when visitors had left the park and the fairies slowly came out of their hiding places – to go for a little splash in the room's own pool with the lightning bugs to the song of the water lily princess from next door.

Peter Weigand

11-Uhr-Nachts RE:RE:AW

Anfangs katastrophal: Gesammelte Kartons als Baumaterial wurden aus Versehen entsorgt. Kein Material konnte die Brandschutzbestimmungen erfüllen, d.h. nach zwei Tagen stand die Gruppe nach wie vor völlig ohne Material da.
Schlaue Gruppe! ... hat auf dem Großmarkt ausrangierte Plexiglas-Oberlichter entdeckt und den zuständigen Kontaktmann gefunden. Damit konnten sie dann das Zimmer bauen... einfache Fügungen, effektiv, weiß-in-weiß und schöne kleine Details wie die rote Wassermelone – natürlich vom Markt! Effekt: supergeil. Oberflächen haben sich gespiegelt und mit der Wölbung verzerrt. Schattenspiel von innen und außen. Großmarkttreiben am Morgen im Kontrast zum Einschlafen in der weißen Blase... aufwachen am anderen Ort, d.h. am gleichen Ort, aber mit völlig anderer Stimmung... Respekt!

In the beginning, there was a catastrophe! Boxes that had been collected as construction material were disposed of. No material would fulfil the fire safety regulations, so after two days, the group was left without any material whatsoever. But this clever group discovered a discarded Plexiglas skylight and found out whom to contact. This was turned into their room: simple joins, white-on-white, and nice little details such as a red watermelon – from the market, of course – resulted in a really cool place. The surfaces reflected each other and were distorted by the vaulting. There was a shadow effect inside and out. Market hall bustle in the morning, rather than the white bubble you went to sleep in... to wake up in another space but in the same place with a completely different atmosphere – respect!

Alexander Römer und David Moritz

Die einzige Gruppe, die wiederholt nicht nur ihren Namen, sondern auch das komplette Konzept umgeworfen hat – und mittlerweile eigentlich 11-Uhr-Nachts heißen will.

This was the only group who not only repeatedly changed their name but also their entire concept. Now they have called it 11-Uhr-Nachts – 11 o'clock in the evening.

Paula Strunden

Das war das einzige Hotelzimmer, das die Jury ohne einen Entwurf ausgewählt hat und zwar, weil es auch der einzige Vorschlag war, direkt mit Menschen aus Mannheim zusammen zu arbeiten. Die beiden Jungs aus Zürich hatten den Kontakt und eine feste Verabredung mit dem Jugendzentrum FORUM Mannheim.
Nach einer lustigen, kollaborativen Planungsphase wurde daraus eine umgebaute Offizierskasinosauna als Hotelzimmer auf den ehemaligen Turley Barracks. Dank der engagierten Jugendlichen bleibt das Zimmer weiterhin in Betrieb.

This was the only hotel room that the jury chose without seeing the design plans because it was the only one that suggested working directly with people from Mannheim. The two men from Zurich were in contact with the FORUM youth centre in Mannheim. After a joyful collaborativ design phase a converted officer's sauna from the Turley barracks became the hotel room. Thanks to the committed young people involved, the room will stay in use.

Benjamin Foerster-Baldenius

Feuer und Flamme

Da gibt es nicht viel zu sagen: sie kamen, sie machten und sie gingen.

There isn't much to say about this team: they came, they constructed, they left.

Lukas Lendzinski

Naja, etwas doch noch: Ohne dieses Team aus Schneeberg in Thüringen und ihrer Explosion aus Feuerwehrschläuchen hätten wir nicht gewusst, dass es in Mannheim keine roten Feuerwehrschläuche gibt. Und wir hätten nicht gewusst, dass es Firmen wie „Firewear" gibt, die uns das Material nachher gerne wieder abnehmen, um es zu recyclen.

Well, perhaps one thing: if it hadn't been for this team from Schneeberg in Thuringia and their explosion of fire brigade hoses, we would never have guessed that Mannheim has no red fire brigade hoses. And we would never have found out that there are firms like Firewear that were willing to take material off our hands once we finished, in order to recycle it.

Benjamin Foerster-Baldenius

Von was träumen die Flaneure unter dem Schiller-Denkmal?

Chikara Fujiwara
Autor und Journalist, Japan

HOTEL shabbyshabby hat es geschafft, uns in alle möglichen Teile Mannheims zu lenken und so die ganze Stadt zur Bühne zu machen. Die Teilnehmer konsumierten die Stadt jedoch nicht als „Touristen“ mit einem klaren Ziel vor Augen, sondern ließen sich vielmehr wie Flaneure durch die Stadt treiben.

Im Passagenwerk unterscheidet Walter Benjamin zwischen „Touristen“ und „Flaneuren“. Der ideale Flaneur unterscheidet sich für Benjamin vom Touristen, der nur die Sehenswürdigkeiten einer Stadt abklappert. Der Flaneur ist eine einsame Existenz, die über eine feinsinnige Wahrnehmung verfügt. Der Flaneur spürt mit eigenen Augen und Schritten die versteckten Geheimnisse der Stadt auf.

Ich habe am Tag vor der Festivaleröffnung an einer geführten Tour mit Benjamin Foerster-Baldenius teilgenommen und mehrere dieser Hotels besichtigt.
Vor den Menschen, die sich auf dem Theaterplatz versammelt hatten, stand ein gut gelaunter Mann mit Zigarette in der einen und einem Megafon in der anderen Hand: „Wer versteht Englisch? Wer Deutsch?“, fragte er und nachdem er die erhobenen Hände überschlagen hatte, sagte er: „Gut, dann spreche ich jetzt auf Englisch“ und begann mit seinem Vortrag. Kurz darauf fing es heftig an zu regnen und der Mann sagte etwas wie: „Liebe Leute! Der Regen ist in einer halben Stunde bestimmt vorbei, bis dahin spendieren wir euch ein Bier, und ihr könnt auch eine Wurst umsonst dazu essen, bleibt also!“ Und tatsächlich wurden wir mit Bier und Würstchen bewirtet und bekamen auch noch Schirme. Was mich aber vor allem überraschte, war, dass Matthias Lilienthal, der künstlerische Leiter des Festivals, selbst die Bierkästen anschleppte und die Flaschen verteilte, wobei sein großer Körper durch die Menge schaukelte. Es herrschte eine unglaublich offene Atmosphäre. Die Teilnehmer der Tour, die wegen des Festivalbeginns eh schon gehobener Stimmung waren, wurden durch Bier und Sekt noch heiterer, und alle fingen an, sich mit ihren bis dahin unbekannten Nachbarn zu unterhalten.

Dreißig Minuten später hörte es tatsächlich auf zu regnen. Die leicht angeschwipste und gut gelaunte große Truppe setzte sich in Bewegung. Wir stiegen auf die Dächer der Gebäude. Wir gingen zu einem Schiff auf dem Fluss. ... Bei dem Hotel, das an Mannheims Haupteinkaufsstraße lag, den Planken, verteilte sich unsere Truppe über die ganze Straße, so dass sogar die Straßenbahn anhalten musste. Aber niemand wurde böse, im Gegenteil, die Leute fragten uns, was wir hier machten, schlossen sich uns an und in einer Art Schneeballeffekt wurden wir immer mehr. Wir ähnelten einer Demonstration. Diese rätselhafte Truppe rief keine lauten politischen Slogans. Aber das Performing Arts Festival bewegte sich durch die Innenstadt, verschmolz mit deren Alltag und bezog viele Bewohner mit ein... ein Phänomen, das mich sehr berührt hat.

Ein paar Tage später bin ich dann allein mit meinem Stadtplan losgezogen und habe mir ein Hotel in einem Außenbezirk Mannheims angesehen. Indem sich die verstreut daliegenden Orte zu einer Figur verbinden, wird die Landschaft der Stadt zu einem dreidimensionalen Gebilde. Es entsteht sogar ein Gefühl der Vertrautheit gegenüber den eher unbekannten Gegenden. Nach der Besichtigung von „Tubheim“, habe ich mich übrigens auf der Suche nach „The Hedonist“ verlaufen und landete in einem türkischen Viertel. Ein für mich als Japaner ungewöhnlicher Geruch von Leben wehte mir entgegen, ein Erlebnis, das ich wohl kaum vergessen werde. Ich hatte das Gefühl, als hätte ich einen Blick auf ein anderes Gesicht der Stadt Mannheim erhascht. Für einen Touristen bedeutet sich zu verirren lediglich den Verlust von Zeit und Kraft, für einen Flaneur aber ist es das Erleben höchsten Glücks, da sich ihm in diesem Moment die Geheimnisse einer ihm unbekannten Stadt offenbaren können.

Glücklicherweise bekam ich noch einen Übernachtungsplatz im „Monumotel". Es lag mitten in der Stadt, am Schillerplatz. In einem kleinen Park steht eine Schiller-Statue, um die ein weißer Vorhang gespannt war. Auf dem auf Pfählen errichten Podest stand ein Bett, direkt unter Schillers Denkmal. Hier sollten die Hotelgäste die Nacht verbringen, bewacht von Schiller mit seinen ausgestreckten Armen.
Am Tag meiner Übernachtung holte ich mir an der Rezeption den Schlüssel und checkte ein. Glücklicherweise war es noch hell, als ich ankam. Ich zog den Schlüssel aus der Eingangstür, eine etwas komplizierte Angelegenheit, und prüfte, wie ich das Zimmer betreten sollte, wobei mich ein paar junge Männer und Frauen beobachteten. „Hi", sprachen sie mich an, „was ist das eigentlich?" Sie wohnten in der Nachbarschaft und hatten sich schon die ganze Zeit gewundert. Ich erklärte es ihnen und fragte: „Wollt ihr reinkommen?" Sie freuten sich und nahmen mein Angebot an. Wir machten ein Erinnerungsfoto unter dem Schiller-Denkmal. Seltsamerweise fühlte ich mich schon wie der Besitzer dieses Zimmers, obwohl ich gerade erst den Schlüssel bekommen hatte.

Es wurde Nacht. Die Nächte in Mannheim sind ruhig. Obwohl sich der Schillerplatz im Zentrum der Stadt befindet, waren kaum Leute zu sehen oder zu hören. Ich hörte einen Mann unbekannter Herkunft an seinem Handy telefonieren, und mir wurde etwas unheimlich. Ich zog leise den Schlüssel ab und verzog mich in mein Zimmer. Dann trat ich auf die Terrasse (in diesem einfachen Hotel gab es nämlich sogar eine Terrasse!) und sah auf den nächtlichen Park hinaus. Es hatte ein wenig zu nieseln begonnen.

Ich trank mein Dosenbier, das ich mir mitgebracht hatte. Wie vornehm, spottete ich über mich selbst und prostete dem Schiller-Denkmal zu. Was für ein seltsames Gefühl! Ich hatte mit diesem Land nicht das Entfernteste zu tun und würde unter einem Denkmal des (im Vergleich zu Deutschen) mir eher unbekannten Friedrich Schiller schlafen. Da ich vorhatte, in seiner Nähe zu nächtigen, wollte ich ihm wenigstens einen kleinen Dank erweisen und schlug bei Wikipedia unter „Schiller" nach. Dort erfuhr ich, dass seine Räuber in Mannheim uraufgeführt worden waren. Ich erfuhr auch, dass bei der Aufführung am 13. Januar 1782 Beifall und Jubelrufe kein Ende fanden und der Legende nach sollen viele Zuschauer vor Begeisterung sogar in Ohnmacht gefallen sein.

Zu meiner Überraschung wachte ich ganz erquickt aus meinem Schlaf auf. Ich hatte allerdings keine Erinnerung daran, was ich geträumt hatte. Vielleicht hatte mein Traum mit Schiller zu tun, vielleicht auch nicht. Es hatte aufgehört zu regnen. Die Luft war klar und im Park waren bereits Mütter mit ihren Kindern sowie ein paar ältere Menschen zu sehen. Ein neuer Tag fing an. Und ich stellte mir vor, wie wahrscheinlich genau im selben Moment ein anderer Gast in einem anderen Zimmer des HOTEL shabbyshabby den Morgen begrüßte.

Normalerweise wird ein Hotel dafür bezahlt, dass es seinen Gästen einen angenehmen Service bietet. Das HOTEL shabbyshabby weicht von diesem allgemeinen Verständnis eines Hotels ab. Und auch die Übernachtungsgäste entsprechen nicht dem in dieser Hinsicht eher passiven Tourismus. Da es keine, wie bei Hotels allgemein übliche Garantie für die „Sicherheit" der Gäste gibt, sind die Männer und Frauen einem Zustand der Verletzbarkeit ausgesetzt, der vulnerability. Diese Verletzbarkeit aber beraubt die Hotelgäste ihrer alltäglichen Identität und ruft etwas in Erinnerung, was in ihnen schlummert. Das können eigene Erinnerungen sein oder auch die Geschichte und Struktur der Stadt. Oder vielleicht die Imagination eines anderen Menschen, der zur selben Zeit an einem anderen Ort die Nacht verbringt.

Auf meinem Bett im „Monumotel" unter dem Schiller-Denkmal lagen zwei rote Kopfkissen. Sicher keine schlechte Wahl für ein frisch verheiratetes Paar, hier eine Nacht der Flitterwochen zu verbringen. Ich habe die Nacht allein hier verbracht. Doch ich konnte nicht umhin mir vorzustellen, wie es wäre, wenn jemand neben mir läge…

What do flâneurs dream of below the Schiller memorial?

Chikara Fujiwara
Author and journalist, Japan

HOTEL shabbyshabby managed to lead us into many different areas in Mannheim, and in doing so, the entire city was turned into a stage. The shabbyshabby participants did not consume the city like tourists with a fixed destination in mind, but instead wandered through it like flâneurs.

In his work The Arcades Project, Walter Benjamin makes the distinction between tourists and flâneurs: The ideal flâneur, in Benjamin's view, is different from the tourist who simply ticks off the city's sights. A flâneur is a lone person, who perceives details and nuance. The flâneur uncovers the city's hidden secrets with his own eyes and ears.

On the day before the festival opened, I joined a guided tour of the city, led by Benjamin Foerster-Baldenius, during which I visited many of these hotels. Our guide turned out to be a cheerful man, who stood in front of the people gathered on the theatre forecourt, a cigarette in one hand, a megaphone in the other. 'Who can speak English? And German?' he asked and once he'd done a hand count: 'Good, I'll speak in English then', before beginning his lecture. Shortly afterwards, there was a heavy rain shower and he said something along the lines of 'Ladies and gentlemen, the rain will probably be over in half an hour, and in that time, we'll treat you to a beer and a sausage – so stay!' And beer and sausages were served, and we were also provided with umbrellas. What surprised me most of all was the fact that Matthias Lilienthal himself, the artistic director of the festival, hauled the heavy beer crates and served the bottles, his large frame swinging through the crowd. There was an incredibly open atmosphere. The tour members, who were in a lively mood due to the start of the festival, only became more jovial after the beer and Sekt, and everyone began talking to whoever happened to be standing next to them.

Half an hour later, it really did stop raining. Our slightly tipsy, cheery troupe set off: we climbed onto the roofs of the buildings, and boarded a riverboat. When we reached the hotel on the Planken, Mannheim's high street, our group spread out across the whole street, forcing even the tram to stop. We received no negative reactions – on the contrary, people asked us what we were doing, joined our group and a kind of snowball effect took place – we grew in size. Soon we looked like a group of demonstrators. But this mysterious ensemble did not shout any political slogans. Instead, the performing arts festival moved through the city centre, fusing with everyday life, and involving many residents – a phenomenon that I found very moving.

A few days later, I set off on my own with a city map and looked at a hotel on the outskirts of Mannheim. The way the scattered sites formed a figure turned the cityscape into a three-dimensional entity: a feeling of familiarity occurred even in unfamiliar districts. After visiting "Tubheim", and in search of "The Hedonist", I lost my way and ended up in a Turkish area. A very unusual smell – for a Japanese person like me – wafted towards me, a sensation I don't think I'll ever forget. I felt as though I had caught a glimpse of a very different Mannheim. For a tourist, losing your way just means wasting time and energy; but for a flâneur, it's pure happiness, a moment when the secrets of a previously unknown city are revealed.

Fortunately I managed to get a bed for the night in the "Monumotel". It was situated right in the city centre on Schillerplatz. A statue of Schiller stands in a small park, around which white drapes had been drawn. On the podium stood a bed erected on stilts, directly below Schiller's memorial. This is where the hotel guests were to spend the

night, watched over by Schiller with his outstretched arms.
When the day of my stay arrived, I picked up the keys from the reception and checked in. Luckily, it was still light when I arrived. I was taking the key out of the door – a rather complicated matter – and was working out how to enter the room, when a few young men and women who were observing me said, 'Hi, what actually is this?' They lived in the neighbourhood and had been puzzling this over for a while. I explained what it was and asked whether they'd like to come in: they were delighted and took up my offer. We took a souvenir photograph underneath the Schiller memorial. Strangely I already felt as if I owned the room, although I'd only just been given the key.

Night fell. Nights in Mannheim are quiet. Although Schillerplatz is in the city centre, barely anyone could be seen or heard. I only caught the conversation of a man talking into his mobile phone, which gave me a creepy feeling. I quietly took the key out of the door and sneaked into my room. Later I stepped out onto the balcony (this simple hotel room even had a balcony!) and looked out across the park at night. A soft drizzle had started.

I drank the can of beer that I had brought with me. How refined, I thought laughing at myself, and drank a toast to the Schiller memorial. What a strange feeling! I didn't have the slightest connection to this country, and was going to spend a night sleeping below Schiller – an unknown personality to me, in comparison to most Germans. As I intended to stay the night next to him, I wanted to at least show a little respect, and looked him up on Wikipedia. There I discovered that The Robbers had premiered in Mannheim. I also discovered that after the performance on 13 January 1782, applause and cheering went on nonstop, and many of the audience members allegedly fainted with enthusiasm.

To my surprise, I woke up quite refreshed the next morning. I couldn't remember, however, what I had dreamed: perhaps it'd had something to do with Schiller, perhaps not. It had stopped raining. The air was clear and in the park, mothers were already out with their children, along with a few older people. A new day started. And I imagined how, at precisely that moment, other guests were waking up in other HOTEL shabbyshabby rooms.

A hotel is normally paid to provide its guests with a pleasant service. A HOTEL shabbyshabby differs from this general understanding of a hotel. And the guests don't correspond to passive tourism either. As there is no guarantee for the guests' safety, as is normally the case in hotels, men and women alike are put in a state of vulnerability. It takes away guests' everyday identities, and wakens a dormant feeling in them: perhaps their own memories, or the history and structure of the city. Or perhaps imagining another person spending the night in another hotel at the same time.

On my bed in the "Monumotel" under the Schiller memorial lay two red pillows. It wouldn't have been a bad spot for a pair of newly-weds to spend their honeymoon night. But I spent the night here alone. On the other hand, I couldn't help imagining how it would have been if someone had been lying next to me…

FANTASTISCH!
fantastisch 30.5.14
I was here! (mary Poppins)
Béla Holme
Und Skafte
Kuhn.
28.05.14
21.05.14
Nacht 0
– there's no distance in between our love –
Sophie
&
Gini
Bye Bye
29.5.14
Lesen, träumen,
dem Klangteppich
lauschen ...
einfach wunderbar.
7.6.14 Eine "heiße" Nacht
auf dem Neckar - gut abgeschirmt
Klein Anton (10 Monate), Anna & Dirk

Idee – toll umgesetzt
Danke an das Umbrella-Team
(50er) 5.6..
Füchse,
Wundergut!
Danke sagen
Jan & Simone
24.5.14
St + Flo
Cool! B.
r werfen nie wieder
n Schirm weg!!!
05.14
abienne + Michèle
Super Schirme
Super Schwäne
Super Spinnen auf dem Klo
SUPERGEIL!
Laura & Julius
So eine Nacht macht süchtig.
Wir wollen nur noch...
Shabby Shabby Shabby
shabby shabby shabby
4.6.14 J+P

Sportsarena

Seit ich mit 16 in der Bravo gelesen habe, dass Boy George in einer Turnhalle wohnt, wollte ich das auch. Als uns die Sportsarea in der US-Army Geisterstadt des Benjamin Franklin Village als Ort für ein Hotelzimmer für HOTEL shabbyshabby angeboten wurde, konnte ich nicht widerstehen. Ya+K hat hier mit Hilfe von drei LKW-Ladungen abgespielter Bühnenbilder des Nationaltheaters Mannheim in kürzester Zeit einen wunderlichen Ort geschaffen. Ein ganzer LKW war allerdings schon alleine für die Giraffe nötig, die sie wie eine Frankensteinpuppe mumifizierten. Alleine in einer leeren Stadt, eingezäunt von Stacheldraht neben dem Kopf einer Giraffenmumie zu schlafen – wer hätte davon nicht schon geträumt?

Ever since I was 16 and read in Bravo magazine that Boy George lived in a gym hall, I have wanted to do the same. So when the sports arena in Benjamin Franklin Village – the ghost town where the US army used to be stationed – was offered to us as a location for HOTEL shabbyshabby, I couldn't resist. In next to no time, Ya+K created a very strange place here with the aid of three truckloads of worn-out set designs from the Nationaltheater Mannheim. One whole truck was needed simply to make the giraffe, which was then mummified like Frankenstein's monster. Sleeping alone in a deserted city, surrounded by barbed wire, and next to the head of a giraffe – who hasn't dreamt of this?

Benjamin Foerster-Baldenius

Ramm Bar Zamm Bar

Eine gute Bar mit einer guten Auswahl an Bieren! Ehrlich gesagt habe ich mit ihnen mehr Bier getrunken als gearbeitet! Ich bin ab und an in der Bauphase vorbeigegangen, aber sie wirkten völlig eigenständig.

The bar was a good bar with a good selection of beer! To be honest I drank more beer than I worked. Somethimes I passed by the bar's construction, but it always seeme completely independent.

Samuel Boche

Schlafen in der Bar? – Dass das nicht geht bei 120 jungen Leuten war ja absehbar.

Sleeping in a bar? That it would be difficult among 120 people was certainly forseeable.

Benjamin Foerster-Baldenius

736

RENA
736

COVAND

samskip
samskip
samskip
MAERSK
MAERSK
Hapag-Lloyd
MOL
HYUNDAI

DB

Impressum

Herausgeber
raumlaborberlin und Theater der Welt 2014 – Ein Festival des Internationalen Theaterinstituts (ITI) in Zusammenarbeit mit Spector Books Leipzig

Texte
Sam Boche, Benjamin Foerster-Baldenius, Chikara Fujiwara, Lukasz Lendzinski, Matthias Lilienthal, David Moritz, Alexander Römer, Heike Schuppelius, Paula Strunden, Peter Weigand

Redaktion
Benjamin Foerster-Baldenius, Paula Strunden, Jan Wenzel

Koordination und redaktionelle Mitarbeit
Katrin Dod

Übersetzung ins Englische / ins Deutsche
Transfiction – die Literaturübersetzer
www.transfiction.eu

Übersetzung aus dem Japanischen
Nora Bierich

Grafik
Chris Rehberger, Jens Paulsen, Julia Egger (DOUBLE STANDARDS)

Zeichnungen
Paula Strunden, raumlaborberlin

Bildbearbeitung
Carsten Humme, Leipzig

Druck
Druckhaus Köthen GmbH & Co. KG

Published by
Spector Books
Harkortstraße 10
04107 Leipzig
Deutschland
Tel. +49 341 264 51 012
Fax +49 341 212 24 11
www.spectorbooks.com

Distribution
USA, Canada: RAM Publications+ Distribution Inc., www.rampub.com
Australia, New Zealand: Perimeter Distribution, perimeterdistribution.com
UK, Japan: Anagram Books Ltd, www.anagrambooks.com
Germany, Austria, Benelux, France: GVA, Gemeinsame Verlagsauslieferung Göttingen GmbH&Co. KG, www.gva-verlage.de
Switzerland: AVA Verlagsauslieferung AG, www.ava.ch
Other countries: Motto Distribution, www.mottodistribution.com

TEAM HOTEL SHABBYSHABBY

Künstlerische Projektleitung
Benjamin Foerster-Baldenius (raumlaborberlin)

Mitdenker / Berater

Lukasz Lendzinski, Peter Weigand (Studio umschichten), Alexander Römer (exyzt/ConstructLab), David Moritz (rocknrollarchitecture), Sam Boche (Bruit du Frigo)

Co-Entwurf und Bauleitung Camp und Festivalzentrum
Florian Stirnemann (raumlaborberlin)

Technische Leitung
Arno Truschinski

Statiker
Joachim Pachmann

Produktionsleitung
Marta Hewelt

Produktionsassistenz
Celine Mentzel

Assistenz
Daniel Sievers

Assistenz raumlaborberlin
Chloé Francou, Paula Strunden

Team Studio umschichten
Coline Robin, Christian Daschek

Leitung Fundraising
Anita Kerzmann

Mitarbeiterin Fundraising
Theresa Rimmele

Aufbauteam
Christian Daschek, Adam Dittrich, Oliver Kachel, Matthias Kolander, Gonzague Lacombe, Coline Robin, Gregor Siems, Malte Stiebritz, Alexej Hermann

Chef de Cuisine
Marius Busch, Kira Kohnen

Jury
Anne Catherine Fleith (Feld72, Wien), Pedro Gadanho (MoMA, New York), Gilly Karjevsky (72 Hour Urban Action, Tel Aviv), Lukasz Lendzinski (Studio umschichten, Stuttgart), Marjetica Potrc (Künstlerin und Architektin, Ljubljana), Alexander Römer (exyzt/constructLab, Paris/Berlin), Benjamin Foerster-Baldenius (raumlaborberlin, Berlin)

Mitarbeit Wettbewerb
Olga Maria Hungar (raumlaborberlin)

Das gesamte Projekt wurde begleitet und veröffentlicht von ARTE Creative http://creative.arte.tv/de

HOTEL shabbyshabby ist ein Projekt von Theater der Welt 2014, raumlaborberlin und ARTE Creative. In Zusammenarbeit mit Studio umschichten (Stuttgart) und ConstructLab (Paris). Gefördert durch die Stadt Mannheim. Ermöglicht durch die großzügige Unterstützung von IKEA Mannheim, Festool Group GmbH, Dorint Kongresshotel Mannheim, engelhorn Mannheim und Gerüstbau Tisch GmbH.

Dank an
Staatliche Rhein-Neckar-Hafengesellschaft Mannheim mnH, Mannheimer Parkhausbetriebe GmbH, GrossMarkt Mannheim GmbH, Jugendkulturzentrum FORUM, Mannheimer Kunstverein e.V., Spedition Knubben, RHM Rohstoff-Handelsgesellschaft mbH MAS Aggregate Service Rheinplus, KFZ Fam. Hesse, Musikpark Mannheim, TIG7, Technoseum Mannheim, Planen Weber, Erdenwerk Mannheim, Permodo, Logistics GmbH, Ernit Flachdach, Feuerwear GmbH & co. KG, Biotopia, Internationaler Bund Mannheim – Gemeinnützige Fahrradwerkstatt.
Stadt Mannheim: Kirsten Batzler, Kulturelle Stadtentwicklung, Waltraud Schlepps, Dr. Konrad Hummel, Geschäftsstelle Konversion, Polizei Mannheim, Feuerwehr Mannheim, Dr. Peter Kurz, Oberbürgermeister der Stadt Mannheim

Besonderer Dank an alle Abteilungen und Mitarbeiter des Nationaltheaters Mannheim, insbesondere an Thomas Busse, Stefan Grießhaber, Regina Silbereis und Nicole Berry sowie an das gesamte Team von Theater der Welt 2014 und den Flaschensammler Markus.

Theater der Welt 2014 ist ein Festival des Internationalen Theaterinstituts (ITI), ausgerichtet vom Nationaltheater Mannheim, gefördert durch die Stadt Mannheim, die Baden-Württemberg Stiftung und die Beauftragte der Bundesregierung für Kultur und Medien.
Unter der Schirmherrschaft von Bundespräsident Joachim Gauck.
Festivalleitung: Burkhard C. Kosminski und Matthias Lilienthal

NTM NATIONAL THEATER MANNHEIM

STADTMANNHEIM²

Baden-Württemberg Stiftung

Die Beauftragte der Bundesregierung für Kultur und Medien

Generalsponsor:

BASF We create chemistry

Printed in Germany

ISBN 978-3-944669-88-5

Bildnachweis/ Picture credits

Adrian Poellinger
116, 117

Alexander Radomski
038

Arthur Bauer
001, 024, 025, 026, 027, 029, 030, 031, 032 l., 033 r., 034, 037, 039, 040 3. Z.l., 040 3. Z.r., 040 3. Z.r., 040 4. Z.l., 040 4. Z.M., 040 4. Z.r., 041 2. Z.l., 041 2. Z.M., 041 3. Z.l., 041 3. Z.r., 041 4. Z.l., 041 4. Z.M., 041 4. Z.r., 042, 043, 044 o., 056 1. Z.l., 056 1. Z.r., 056 2. Z.l., 056 2. Z.M., 056 3. Z.r., 056 4. Z.l., 058, 059, 060, 061, 066, 067, 069, 072, 067 r., 078, 079, 082, 083, 084, 085, 086, 090, 091 o., 091 u., 095, 096, 097, 098, 099, 106, 107, 114, 120, 121, 136 o.l., 136, 137, 138, 139, 143, 144, 145, 146, 147

Benjamin Foerster-Baldenius
028 u.l., 056 3. Z.l., 056 4. Z.r., 148

CaneHarry-C-y
132, 133

Celine Mentzel
044

Chloé Francou
028 o.l., 057, 080, 081

Christian Kleiner, NTM
022, 023, 032 r., 033 l., 036, 040 2. Z l., 046, 052, 053, 054, 056 2. Z.r., 062, 063, 070, 071, 072, 073, 092, 092, 093, 102, 124, 125

Jugendforum Mannheim
118, 119

Klaus Rothenhöfer
017

Pascal Osten
040 2. Z.M., 142

Paula Strunden
047, 094, 100, 101, 122 l., 122 r., 130, 131

Rudolf Stricker
134, 135

Samuel Boche
040 1. Z.l., 040 1. Z.M., 040 1. Z.r., 040 2. Z.r., 041 1. Z.l., 041 1. Z.M., 041 1. Z.r., 041 2. Z.r., 041 3. Z.M.

Team For'rest
055

Team Hotel Carl
064, 065, 065 r.u.

Team Monumotel
068

Team Stadtloge
087

Team Fairy Tank
089, 104, 105

Team 11-Uhr-Nachts
112, 113

raumlaborberlin Spector Books